EXLIBRIS

CATECHESIS OF REVELATION

Studies in Religious Education

Edited by
Gerard S. Sloyan
Head, Department of Religious Education
The Catholic University of America

Catechesis
of Revelation

Gabriel Moran, F.S.C.

HERDER AND HERDER

1966
HERDER AND HERDER NEW YORK
232 Madison Avenue, New York 10016

Library of Congress Catalog Card Number: 66–22607
© 1966 by Herder and Herder, Inc.
Manufactured in the United States of America

Contents

Introduction

In a previous book in this series I proposed that a theology of revelation carries within itself important principles for catechetical work.[1] In the present volume I intend to sketch out in some detail this interrelationship of theology and catechetics. The order and perspective remain theological, but the purpose is now overtly pastoral. My procedure is to a large extent deductive, asking what should be the effect upon catechetical theory supposing that the previous theological analysis of revelation has been correct.

It should be said immediately, however, that this relationship between theory and practice, or between the theological and catechetical, is not unilateral. If the catechist has much to learn from the theologian, the converse is also true. Indeed, one of the reasons for my confidence in expounding theologically derived principles for catechetics is that I have found an immediate resonance when experienced catechists have listened to them and have in turn tried to explain what they are doing. Many of the ideas in these pages, therefore, are already being used by large numbers of religion teachers. Yet the impression one receives is that some of these teachers are doing their job with a tinge of regret or a guilty conscience. They would like to teach all about Christian revelation, but they feel that it is impossible under the circumstances. Instead, they are doing their best trying to make

[1] *Theology of Revelation* (New York, Herder and Herder, 1966).

the students' Christian lives intelligible by any means that are available. Part of my task in this book will be to show that the direction which has already been taken by some of these experienced catechists is not only allowed but is demanded by a thoroughly understood theology of revelation. I hope to show that these tendencies are not based solely upon the psychological or moral deficiencies of the students, but are supported by the nature of Christian revelation itself.

It is imperative that the task of relating theology of revelation to catechetics be carried out, and this for two main reasons. First, teachers who intuitively sense what must be done in the teaching of religion should be given some confidence in and some insight into what they are doing. Psychology has been of considerable help here, and for this one must be grateful to the psychologists. However, the chief contributor to the development of catechetical theory ought surely to be theology. Unfortunately, there is some indication that many teachers of religion sense a conflict between psychological and theological approaches to the teaching of religion. Faced with a widening split between these two, the teachers will tend to opt in practice for the first while struggling to hold on to the second. The solution to the catechist's dilemma is not to ask him to prefer theology over psychology, but to provide him with a better theological understanding of his work. A battle waged between, on the one hand, advocates of a psychologically oriented teaching that makes use of students' needs and desires, and on the other hand advocates of a scriptural-theological approach to teaching, would be an inexcusable tragedy.

The second main reason for this work is the need to distinguish between the legitimate and well-founded adaptations made by competent religion teachers, and the superficial and perhaps harmful changes made by those lacking sufficient grasp either of Christian revelation or of the function of teaching. Some competent and well-trained teachers of religion have abandoned the textbook for the newspaper and the Bible. But the fact that a teacher has jettisoned much or all of the old structure is by no means a proof that he is up-to-date in his teaching and is skilled in the conveyance of Christian revelation. A lack of unity and organization in the teaching of religion is not something particularly to be prized. In both Catholic schools and in Confraternity programs, there has developed very rapidly a startling variety of individual approaches to the teaching of religion. The difference between what is listed in the syllabus and what is now going on in the actual teaching situation is far greater than many administrators are either aware of or are admitting. This grass-roots development is ambivalent. Insofar as it represents a breakdown of unifying structure it is a temporary disruption that is potentially a great threat to the work of catechizing. On the other hand, this development represents one of the primary sources for a better understanding of the catechetical mission of the Church. People who write on catechetics and people who construct syllabuses ought to listen to the people who do the catechizing. At any rate, the somewhat frightening collapse of tightly organized systems of religion teaching cannot be corrected by a heavy hand coming down from above to insist that the old way be restored. We cannot go back to the old way because there is nothing to go back to. The new bases of unity and organization must emerge from the experience of teachers together with an understanding provided by a solid scriptural-theological knowledge.

Part One

Part One

I.

The Catechetical Problem

To guarantee that our changes in religious education today are not haphazardly made but are based upon Christian principles, we need to elaborate a strong theological basis for these changes.[1] Most central to this undertaking is the area which I have called the theology of revelation. Here I will recapitulate some of the main themes which are developed in *Theology of Revelation* and which will appear throughout this work.

I have tried to show that Christian revelation is a personal communion of knowledge, an interrelationship of God and the individual within a believing community. God's bestowal and man's acceptance are both indispensable to the process. The human partner is not a recipient of "something" called revelation. Humanity stands within the process and not outside of it, and revelation is not a "thing" at all but exists only in present, continuing, conscious experience of people, that is, in the relation of God and his people. In this perspective, the humanity of Jesus Christ is not just an instrument or a visual aid through which God communicates his truths. Jesus is the main recipient

[1] See Bernard Cooke, "Theology and Catechetical Renewal," in *Pastoral Catechetics*, edited by Johannes Hofinger and Theodore Stone (New York, Herder and Herder, 1964), pp. 88–104; see also Alfonso Nebreda, *Kerygma in Crisis* (Chicago, Loyola University Press, 1965), p. 66; Lewis Sherrill, *Gift of Power* (New York, Macmillan, 1955), p. 68.

13

of God's self-gift, and it is in the consciousness of Jesus that God is most perfectly known. In his life, and definitively in his death-resurrection, revelation reaches a high point never to be diminished. With the resurrection of Christ and the sending of the Spirit, revelation *begins* in fullness.

The Church of believers opening out toward the whole of mankind is the place where God is now revealing himself. The Church understands this continuing revelation through the awareness of herself as the Body of Christ. She meditates upon God manifested in Christ with the help of her whole tradition and most particularly with the eyewitness testimony of the apostles. Revelation ceases with Christ but Christ has not ceased. He continues to be the mediator of God and man and in such a way that all of mankind and creation is affected by his high priesthood. Everything in creation thus takes on the capability of being a revelatory instrument of God, but by the same reasoning nothing of itself can be guaranteed to be a revelatory instrument.

These ideas are implicit throughout Catholic tradition, though it is only recently that some of them have emerged into clear focus.[2] Much of Catholic teaching is formulated in the language of "revealed truths" stored in a deposit. There is a legitimate basis for this use of language, but it must nevertheless be kept subordinate to the primary reality here: God now revealing himself to man in Jesus Christ.

Catechetical and liturgical writing, strangely enough, has outstripped theology in the recognition that revelation must be a present, personal, social happening if it is to mean anything to our world. Catechetics and liturgy have been using the right words in saying that God reveals himself to the present com-

[2] The *Constitution on Divine Revelation* from the Second Vatican Council represents a summary of many of these developments. This document is the fruit of at least a century of scriptural and theological study. Far from rejecting tradition, these recent studies have largely been a regrounding of theology in the biblical, patristic, and medieval sources.

14

munity. Unfortunately, there has not been enough underpinning to the words being used. When pressed at all by critics, catechetical writers have hastened to affirm their orthodoxy by saying that they do not of course mean the divine public revelation which was finished when "St. John put down his pen."[3] As a result, catechetical writing is taken to be a collection of pious metaphors that cannot be defended theologically. The fact of the matter is, however, that the supposed metaphors are more accurate theologically than the very inadequate understanding of revelation found in many theology manuals. Catechetical theory cannot advance by putting pious patches onto old inadequate definitions of revelation. It must demand a better theology of revelation, one which brings out the present, personal, social character of God revealing in Christ.

Not only is the theorizing of catechetical writers involved here, but also more practical issues concerning Catholic schools and CCD, educational policies and financial investments, child and adult education. These are obviously complex problems with many factors to be considered. I would suggest, however, that it is not irrelevant to raise the theological question of revelation instead of assuming that everybody understands and agrees upon the general task entailed by Christian revelation, so that the only differences would be in regard to methods of implementation. In many disagreements over the role of the schools and the possibility of radical change, there are different assumptions made about the nature of revelation and the possibility of its conveyance to another. These assumptions are seldom what is argued.[4] A theo-

3 Gerald Emmet Carter, *The Modern Challenge to Religious Education* (New York, Sadlier, 1961), p. 169.

4 This was so particularly in the controversy caused by Mary Perkins Ryan, *Are Parochial Schools the Answer?* (New York, Holt, Rinehart and Winston, 1964). In her article, "To My Critics," in *Ave Maria* (May 23, 1964), pp. 14–15, 25–26, the author pointed to the basic theological issue that she was trying to raise in the book, but this issue was practically never discussed in the many criticisms of the book. For a summary of reactions to

15

logical reflection on the foundations of religious education would not resolve the controversies in this area, but it could perhaps reveal where some of the real differences lie. Thus the theology could contribute to bringing about a better formulation of the arguments than has hitherto been possible. For example, this book does not advocate an increase of money and manpower for adult education; in fact, most of the book deals with the education of children because that is the way things now are. However, if one accepts the theology of revelation and the catechetical consequences indicated here, this book might well lead one to conclude that the focus of religion teaching ought to be shifted away from children toward the adult world.

In *Theology of Revelation* I disavowed the claim that theology would of itself be adequate for answering questions of catechetical theory. Indeed, what should have become very clear there is the importance of the human sciences as indicated by the theology of revelation itself. Contrary to superficial presentations which assume that revelation is something that is "outside" man and must be placed "inside" him, I have tried to show that revelation is a personal relationship being participated in by the Jewish community, by the man Jesus, and by every man who lives today in the continuing revelation of the Church. In this context, the study of the human person is helpful and necessary not for finding ways to get the revelation inside man or to adapt the teachings of revelation to contemporary man. Instead, the study of man should be the illumination of revelation itself insofar as revelation happens in the life of man and nowhere else. This is not to deny a distinction between faith and reason, the supernatural and the natural. Grace remains grace, but according to Catholic doctrine, grace

the book, see Ronald Luka, "Special Review: Are Parochial Schools the Answer?," in *American Ecclesiastical Review*, CLI (October, 1964), pp. 271–277.

16

does not replace nature or build something on top of nature. God in his gracious design took hold of man and transformed his concrete, historical existence. Modern knowledge from fields such as psychology or sociology is not to be identified with Christian revelation. On the other hand, it is equally false merely to juxtapose human scientific knowledge and Christian revelation as if there were no inner relationships. A theology of revelation must be developed in such a way that it is left open to enrichment from other fields of study. Theology of revelation is of immense importance for establishing catechetical foundations, but it cannot pretend to be exhaustive of the analysis needed here. This study, therefore, would fail its purpose if it did not indicate the need for continuing research in the psychology of a child's religious development and the sociological factors in religious belief.[5]

I have not attempted here to work out all the detailed catechetical applications that could be made from the theological study. There is no question of working out a practical methodology embodying that theology. Neither is there any attempt made to trace the religious development of the child and his relation to revelation at various stages of his growth. The most that I can do is to refer to such an evolution while leaving analysis of its development to other studies.

What I do propose to do is to examine some of the commonly held principles of recent catechetical writing from the viewpoint of a theology of revelation. That a principle is true does not guarantee that it is thoroughly understood by those who enunciate it. Even less does it mean that the principle is not open to

[5] There can be little doubt that we stand in great need of empirical studies in these areas; see Orlo Strunk, *Religion: A Psychological Interpretation* (New York, Abingdon Press, 1962), p. 103: "The 'objective' measures we have used to date invalidate, for the most part, our conclusions, and certainly bring into serious doubt the belief that we understand religious behavior at all."

further development by being probed theologically. These reflections would be worth-while even were I to find myself in agreement with most of what is being written or assumed in catechetical circles today. In fact, however, there are key points at which I shall take issue with some widely stated principles that I believe are at least ambiguous or badly stated if not erroneous.

David Hunter has suggested[6] that we need to go through four steps in the improvement of religious education. He says that we must: (1) understand the situation giving rise to the need; (2) identify the real dynamisms of the situation; (3) develop a strategy for coming to grips with the dynamic forces; (4) plan tactics and procedures. Hunter contends that we constantly jump from the first to the fourth of these stages, whereas the main work lies in between them. I would like to think that the present work lies somewhere between the second and third of his stages. It should contribute toward understanding the dynamisms involved in catechetics though it does not reach an over-all strategy or detailed procedure.

This admitted limitation may be disappointing to those who want a detailed program of instruction. I have almost nothing to say on drawing up a program of instruction, not because I think this unimportant but because I think it is impossible to come to grips with this issue in works such as the present one. This is particularly true when the theological dynamisms of the catechetical mission are not sufficiently understood. Even if they were understood, I should not think that the tactics and procedures should become the center of discussion. Contrary to what is often said today, our chief need is not detailed programs and more practical applications for religion teachers. We ought to stop attempting to create these *a priori* because we always end up with the pseudo-concrete, the pseudo-practical, new frustrations

[6] See *Christian Education as Engagement* (Greenwich, Seabury Press, 1963), pp. 32–33.

and more disappointments. Only when we have given up all hope of solving our catechetical problem with cut-rate answers and we begin to search for a deeper understanding will we eventually get more practical answers. These will ultimately be worked out by the people who teach and the people who learn, not by the people who write books on catechetics. Before taking up the main theological areas it will be profitable in the following two chapters to situate the present catechetical problem against the background of an emerging theology of revelation.

II.

Recent Developments

IT is a remarkable fact that the year 1936 is cited in so many places as a turning point in the history of Catholic religious education, and this for one main reason: the publication of Josef Jungmann's *The Good News and Our Proclamation of the Faith*.[1] Of course, like all foundation-shaking books, this one did not drop down out of the heavens without warning. It was the fruit of many years of preparation both within the Church and within the life and work of the author. What I wish to follow here, however, is neither the historical development previous to this book nor the lengthy debates which this book engendered in the 1930's and 1940's.[2] I wish only to show that there gradually arose from these many books and articles the realization of a need to ask more ultimate questions about the nature of Christian revelation itself. Although Jungmann did not pose the problem in these theoretical terms, his pastoral and

[1] This was published in abbreviated form in English translation as *The Good News Yesterday and Today* (New York, Sadlier, 1962).

[2] A summary of these debates may be found in Domenico Grasso, *Proclaiming God's Message* (Notre Dame, University of Notre Dame Press, 1965), pp. xvi–xxi; Josef Jungmann, "Theology and Kerygmatic Teaching," in *Lumen Vitae*, V (April, 1950), pp. 258–263; for extensive bibliography on the question, see Emil Kappler, *Die Verkündigungstheologie* (Freiburg, Schweiz, Paulusverlag, 1949), pp. 22–28.

historical considerations have reverberated within theology and have given impetus to a more thorough study of revelation.

Jungmann's analysis of the contemporary problem of preaching and catechizing may be briefly summarized.[3] Jungmann bemoaned the lack of deep understanding of Christian revelation among Catholic people. He claimed that although there is adherence to doctrines and moral precepts, there is little appreciation of the dynamism, unity, and joy which should characterize Christian faith. Conventional Christianity, he claimed, with its beliefs and devotional practices sustained by a Church dominated milieu, is no longer possible. Thus, Christian faith will tend to wither away in the face of modern man's outlook on the universe unless the structure inherent in Christian revelation is subjectively assimilated by the masses of Christian people. Our times demand a greater concentration, a return to the sources of power, a preaching of the gospel to people whose religious knowledge is for the most part a collection of bits and pieces, without unity, coherence, or hierarchical structure. He did not propose, however, the teaching of some vast, logical synthesis of doctrine. On the contrary, he claimed that this is what we have been attempting and that this is what constitutes a large part of our problem. What he did propose was that the important things be said and that they be said well and that they be said often, that real problems of real people be discussed, and that Christian motivation be the basis for all moral exhortation.

The only way that this program could be accomplished was by a refocusing of attention upon the center of Christian revelation as found in Scripture and liturgy, and by a turning away from the peripheral elements that clutter up modern catechisms. Jungmann directed attention to the earliest examples of Christian preaching and teaching as they are found in the Acts of the

[3] The following material is taken largely from Jungmann, *The Good News Yesterday and Today*, chapters 1–5.

Apostles.[4] The style and the content of these sermons are strikingly different from the style and content of modern preaching. The apostolic discourses were mainly concerned with presenting the history of God's dealing with mankind, that is, the preparatory phase of the Old Testament, the historical culmination in Jesus Christ, and the present working of God in the history of the New Israel.

This awareness of the historical reality of Christian revelation as communicated through Bible and liturgy is manifest in the Apostolic Church and throughout the patristic age.[5] No clear line of division can be made to indicate when this sense of the historical was lost. The Bible and the liturgy retained central roles after St. Augustine and up into the Middle Ages, but the sense of revelation as a history gradually diminished. In the later Middle Ages and in the post-Reformation era, there was a striking absence of the historical dimension in the presentations of theology and catechetics. When a concern did grow up for historical research it was directed more to ascertaining the immobility of doctrines and practices than to discerning the process of historical evolution and the present actuality of revelation.[6]

The real significance of this loss of the sense of historical progress, as Jungmann went on to show, is that it was symbolic

---

[4] See particularly Acts 2, 3, 10; for a study of these discourses, see C. H. Dodd, *The Apostolic Preaching and Its Developments* (3rd edition; London, Hodder and Stoughton, 1963), pp. 7–35; also Domenico Grasso, "The Core of Missionary Preaching," in *Teaching All Nations*, edited by Johannes Hofinger (New York, Herder and Herder, 1961), pp. 39–58.

[5] See Walter J. Burghardt, "Catechetics in the Early Church: Program and Psychology," in *Living Light*, I (Autumn, 1964), p. 109; "For the Fathers, religious instruction is a concrete, living, thrilling thing. Christian doctrine, God's message of salvation, is transmitted and made effective in a twin context and by twin instruments: Scripture and liturgy. Briefly, God's message through God's word and God's action. Better, God's word through God's action in history and in mystery."

[6] See Alan Richardson, *History Sacred and Profane* (Philadelphia, Westminster, 1964), pp. 78–79.

of a general move away from the real. In place of a personal, present, social revelation in the history of a people, there was gradually substituted a revelation conceived in terms of static and objective categories. Given this change, the unity of Christian revelation is not found in the person of Jesus Christ and those who live in union with him, but instead the unity of Christian belief becomes that of the abstract system. "Everything fits together, then, to give us the image of a strictly logical, soulless, secularized Christendom. Instead of a Savior of the world we find the idea of an appearance of God among men, come to teach and win their love; the Church is the organization for preaching this doctrine; and as for the sacraments, there is the possibility of the remission of sins—and the puzzling assistance of grace for the performance of moral obligations."[7]

Jungmann's complaint about the inadequacy of preaching and catechizing was not so new as the reasons he gave for our present predicament and the remedies he seemed to be proposing. He suggested that our catechisms are poor because they are summaries of seminary manuals, and our preaching inadequate because it is directly derived from the "school theology." Instead of attacking this theology, however, Jungmann defended its role in seeking the truth of Christian revelation, but he asserted that this was to be distinguished from the Church's pastoral work concerned with Christian living and the value of revelation. *"Theology is primarily at the service of knowledge;* hence it investigates religious reality to the outermost limits of the knowable (*verum*) and struggles here for the last little piece of truth that can be grasped, without asking in each instance about the significance such effort may have for life."[8] Thus one should expect that theology would concern itself with dissecting revelation into numerous premises

[7] Jungmann, *The Good News Yesterday and Today,* p. 55.
[8] *Ibid.,* p. 33.

23

and conclusions, would concentrate on the peripheral elements of revelation, would extend itself in defending various points of doctrine against heretical intrusions. However, clarifying what is heretical and what is not heretical does not necessarily mean that the Christian life has been clarified; protecting Catholic doctrine is not the same as answering the needs of Catholic peoples.

On the surface, Jungmann was merely asking for a reorientation of pastoral efforts and a greater emphasis upon Scripture and liturgy. Implicit in these proposals, however, was a challenge to theology, a challenging of the fundamental content, framework, and methodology of modern theology. It was, in short, a questioning of whether modern theology had really come to grips with the nature of revelation. If Christian revelation is historically, biblically, and liturgically centered, if it is a living, actual, communal reality, if it is fulfilled and summarized in the person of Christ, then the logical question to ask was why theology did not seem to have these qualities.

Proposing a presentation of revelation in preaching and catechizing that radically differed from standard theological presentations would seem to imply one of the following alternatives: (1) theology is true to the nature of revelation, but revelation must then be pragmatically adjusted to fit the needs of piety; (2) theology cannot cope with the nature of revelation, but must itself remain peripheral in scope and take second place to more concrete and practical considerations of revelation; (3) theology can be true to the nature of revelation and closely related to pastoral work, but in fact to become so it is in need of drastic revision and deep rethinking. The first of these possibilities would hardly be acceptable to anyone and does not seem consonant with the whole Catholic tradition. On the other hand, neither the second nor the third could be very appealing to theologians. Whichever alternative was taken, a serious challenge was thereby issued to Catholic theology. It is hardly surprising that a strong reaction among Catholic theologians was not long in coming.[9]

A lively controversy before and after World War II ensued upon Jungmann's proposals. To some people it seemed clear that a new kind of study—a scriptural, liturgical, non-scholastic, "kerygmatic" theology—must be developed to supplement the scientific theology of the schools that was inadequate for pastoral needs. To others it seemed that this attempt to develop a "kerygmatic theology" would only exacerbate the situation; what was needed, they asserted, was not less theology but more theology, not a non-scientific theology but a theology more deeply and truly scientific. On the surface, these two positions were diametrically opposed to one another. Actually, there was a good deal of agreement that tended to be obscured by the fact that the two were not speaking to the same question. As one commentator summarized it: "Utz—and this is the case with nearly all the opponents of the kerygmatic theology—remains on the level of principles and necessities: what theology ought to be. [Hugo] Rahner—and all the Kerygmatics—are situated at the level of fact, how theology has historically developed. There are differences in the focus of concern; but no opposition in what is affirmed."[10] Yves Congar described the controversy in similar terms. He pointed out that the "kerygmatics" started from the fact experienced by nearly all priests, namely, the radical split between what they were given in the schools of theology and what they find they need for carrying out the work of their ministry.[11]

[9] See Domenico Grasso, "The Good News and the Renewal of Theology," in Jungmann, The Good News Yesterday and Today, pp. 204–205.

[10] Andrés A. Esteban Romero, "La controversia en torno a la teología kerigmática," in XV Semana Española de Teología (Madrid, 1956), p. 384.

[11] See "Bulletin de théologie dogmatique," in Revue des sciences philosophiques et théologiques, XXV (1951), p. 591.

There was, then, both much agreement on the present pastoral difficulty of the Church and also much difference of opinion on the role to be played by traditional, scientific theology in meeting contemporary needs. Those defending the pastoral importance of a scientific theology had to plead for time until their science could be enriched with new biblical, liturgical, and historical knowledge. The "kerygmatics," on the other hand, were more concerned with the immediate problem and the need to revitalize preaching and catechizing without delay. Their plan was clear: they intended to awaken Christians to those things which are most central to faith, they wanted to place Christ at the center of God's salvific history, they wanted to bring men to respond to the central values of Christian revelation.

With these admirable ends one could hardly be in disagreement; nevertheless, in the thinking of many theologians, the questions were more complex than the kerygmatic enthusiasts were willing to admit. Their sharp contrasts exposed their position to attack and sometimes to caricature. For example, a distinction between a theology of the true and a theology of the good could not be pushed very far without it appearing to be simplistic.[12] Formulations like this, however, were not the main issue. The fundamental question was this: Whether the simple, meaningful presentation of revelation in the sources of Christian faith could and should be kept separate from the rational reflection of theology, or whether a theology which understands its purposes and limitations could bring out the deeper significance of an historical, personal, and social revelation while remaining true to the spirit of the Bible, the prayerful attitude of the liturgy, and the inherent structure of revelation itself.

The theology of revelation implicit throughout Catholic tradition could leave little doubt that the latter position must ulti-

---

[12] See Grasso, *Proclaiming God's Message,* p. xxviii; Congar, "Bulletin de théologie dogmatique," *loc. cit.,* p. 599.

mately be the correct one. Thus it did come about that those who advocated the development of a "kerygmatic theology" to be placed next to a scientific theology eventually lost the battle. They did succeed, however, in making a firm impression upon the theology which has followed. The formulation of a separate "kerygmatic theology" is now generally rejected, but the vital character of theology that the "kerygmatics" were seeking is just as generally accepted.[13]

Those theologians who had defended the central place of scientific theology had not for the most part denied the aridity of much of the school theology. What they did deny was the assertion or the implication that theology in itself had to be that way. They wished to distinguish between the inadequate or outdated theology that had become solidified in many manuals and theology as such. They insisted that it is a dangerous thing to attack theology and that the attempt to get rid of theology necessarily introduces bad theology. Every adult who gives the least thought to his Christian life is already practicing theology in one way or another.[14]

These theologians maintained that despite the good intentions of their kerygmatic opponents, much of the effort was misdirected. There was a dangerous implication that intellectual reflection upon revelation is at best irrelevant and at worst detrimental to living in revelatory communion with God.[15] They maintained, therefore, that what was needed was not a "purer"

[13] See Josef Jungmann, *Handing on the Faith* (New York, Herder and Herder, 1959), p. 399.

[14] See Michael Schmaus, *Katholische Dogmatik* (München, Hueber, 1960), I, p. 23; M. D. Chenu, *Is Theology a Science?* (New York, Hawthorn Books, 1959), p. 18.

[15] See Bernard Cooke, "The Problem of Sacred Doctrine in the College," in *Modern Catechetics,* edited by Gerard S. Sloyan (New York, Macmillan, 1963), p. 283; Gerard S. Sloyan, "The Relation of the Catechism to the Work of Religious Formation," *ibid.,* p. 95.

revelation uncontaminated by theology, but a revelation deeply reflected upon by human beings. What was needed was not a non-scientific study of revelation, but a study of revelation so deeply scientific that it would become pastoral, practical, and relevant.[16] The only sufficient proof of this thesis would be in the actual production of theological works that fulfill these conditions. While one would hesitate to make definitive judgments about the last few decades of theologizing, it seems safe to say that there has been shown the possibility for a revitalization of every part of Catholic theology.

Theologians have come to realize the possibility and the need to break through some of the rigid structures which had grown up in Catholic theology and which were not a part of theology as such. This has been done not by overthrowing or destroying medieval and post-Tridentine theology, but by going to the roots of all theology, by rethinking the development of Christian truth, and by preserving the best that has been produced in every era while making use of contemporary thought forms. Instead of assuming that the "truths of revelation" are obvious and that the main work is the reasoning to conclusions from the *articula fidei,* theologians have begun to probe more deeply into the nature of revelation itself. This, of course, was not entirely new. There have always been theologians who realized that theology is not a science of drawing theological conclusions, but that theological

[16] See Paul Hitz, "Théologie et catéchèse," in *Nouvelle revue théologique,* LXXVII (November, 1955), pp. 916–923; Karl Rahner, "The Student of Theology: The Problem of his Training Today," in *Theology for Renewal* (New York, Sheed and Ward, 1965), p. 137: "A more unambiguously pastoral orientation of theology towards testifying to and proclaiming the Faith to people as they really are today would compel a deepening of it: and this means ultimately a real increase in 'scholarliness,' a 'scholarship' which would not indeed need to be imposed on theological students but would have to have been achieved beforehand at the professors' level in theological research. It would quickly appear that a genuinely 'kerygmatic theology' calls for *more* scholarship on the part of the teacher, who then needs to demand correspondingly less on the part of his pupils."

conclusions are only a means to a radical reflection upon the revelation itself.[17]

When theology is carried out in this way, that is, as a fully scientific yet prayerful reflection upon the whole of God's revelation, then any chasm between theology and catechetics disappears. The two do remain distinct and for that reason there can be a fruitful exchange between them. Theology becomes useful to the pastoral life of the Church by first of all being true to itself as theology. "For a true theology of proclamation is nothing else than the one theology, which takes its religious task so seriously with all the scientific means at its disposal, that it becomes at once more scientific and more kerygmatic."[18]

Thus Catholic theology has made much progress toward a self-renewal which is enabling it to be of service to the pastoral life of the Church. There is still room, however, for more examining of ultimate foundations. The task of understanding the self-disclosure of God in Christ in the present life of the Church has been accomplished only in fragmentary form.[19] Not until there is reached a full understanding of revelation as a present, personal, conscious, free happening with Christ and our brothers in society will the full interrelation of theology and catechetics become evident. Only by making use of the resources now available for a development of the theology of revelation will the catechetical enterprise become fully clear.

[17] See Emile Mersch, *Theology of the Mystical Body* (St. Louis, B. Herder, 1951), pp. 27–46; see also Chenu, *op. cit.,* pp. 48–99.

[18] Karl Rahner, "Current Problems in Christology," in *Theological Investigations* (Baltimore, Helicon, 1961), I, p. 200; see also Gerard S. Sloyan, "Seminary Training and Religious Education," in *Modern Catechetics,* p. 298.

[19] See Charles Davis, "Theology and Its Present Task," in *Theology and the University,* edited by John Coulson (Baltimore, Helicon, 1964), p. 110.

III.

The Present Situation

IN the previous chapter I have chiefly been concerned with the effect upon theology of Jungmann's work and the works that followed in its wake. The more direct effect may be seen in the literature on preaching and catechizing which found a direction for itself and a new vocabulary to express itself. Jungmann had called for a concentration upon the central elements of Christian revelation as summarized in the sermons of the Acts of the Apostles, that is, in the kerygma. Slightly more than a decade later, André Rétif could sum up the movements within missionary and apostolic fields by saying: "*Le kerygme est à la mode.*"[1] It took a few more years for this development to spread throughout America, but by now there are few religion teachers in this country who have not heard of the "kerygmatic approach" to teaching religion. The movement and its name have become widely known, but this does not necessarily mean that the task of the religion teacher has become crystal clear.

Throughout the catechetical literature now available in this

[1] See *Foi au Christ* (Paris, Les Editions du Cerf, 1953), p. 7; It should be noted that the so-called "kerygmatic approach" to teaching religion is to be distinguished from the "kerygmatic theology" movement. Although the two are obviously related, the former has a much broader connotation in referring to a scriptural-liturgical orientation in religion teaching. It does not necessarily imply the thesis of a separate "kerygmatic theology" that we treated in the last chapter.

country there would seem at first sight to be a strong consensus on what the object of catechetical work is and what must be done to achieve it. Not only is there agreement on the essential aims and instruments of catechetics, but there is also a striking similarity of vocabulary throughout this writing. This convergence of principles, ideas, and terminology would seem to be indicative of one of two things. It could mean that the problems of religious education have now been grasped and formulated with great precision. Our task would then be to work out more detailed answers and get these circulated around the country. I would like to believe that this is the case, but I suspect that it is not so. Instead, the alternative possibility is more likely to be true, namely, that the principles most confidently and most frequently repeated in catechetical writing today are rather vague and negative generalities which prove only that the decisive issues are not yet clear in our minds. As Rahner has several times remarked, what is put forward as a summons to action may be only a general principle, and statements verbally the same may change from prescriptions to abstractions.[2]

When religion teaching was first being brought under careful scrutiny and when many people were coming to the conclusion that all was not well with religious education, it was not difficult to make a broad, sweeping attack upon what was going on in the schools and churches. Those who echoed Jungmann's call for criticism and renewal eventually received widespread support for their demands. In fact, there is practically no one associated with religious education today who would say that he advocates rationalism instead of living faith, that he prefers legalism to personal commitment, that he wants meaningless catechism answers rather than a relevant Christian message. The only trouble with this statement of aims is that unless one goes more

[2] See *The Dynamic Element in the Church* (New York, Herder and Herder, 1964), p. 31.

31

deeply into the matter, the second half of each of these pairs is simply the negation of the first. Despite appearances to the contrary, these formulas express much more clearly what we are opposed to than what we are in favor of. Of course, there is a place for these formulas in the examination of our catechetical problems; unfortunately, however, the negative generalities have often been propagated not as the call for a renewal (which they are), but as the renewal itself (which they are not). As a result, the catechetical movement has not been taken seriously in some quarters.

The catechetical movement has from its inception hovered on the brink of trivialization; it continues to hang there. It will never be accepted as more than a realignment of tactics, a redefining of technical words, a reassessment of methodological gimmicks, unless it incorporates into itself the best that is available in fields such as philosophy, anthropology, and psychology. It must wrestle with the exegesis of Scripture and deal with the history of the Church. At the very least, catechetics ought to recognize that theology is its chief ally and not an enemy or an estranged relative. It is time to put to definitive rest the implication that theological reflection upon Christian faith is mostly irrelevant and perhaps a bit dangerous to the Christian life. Some catechetical writing seems to be oblivious of what has been going on for the past thirty years in theology. Such a position is difficult to understand considering the role of theology in the Second Vatican Council. Theology is not an irrelevant game being played by professors; it is the driving force in the Church today that will make or break any catechetical movement.

Advances in religion teaching have, in fact, come about through the influence of improved theology. However, the effect has not been greater because of a simplistic opposition between theology and catechetics that still pervades catechetical writing. For example, the statement is often made in catechetical literature that theology deals mainly with "doctrine" but that catechetics is concerned with the "message." There is a difference between theology and catechetics that is vaguely hinted at by this terminology, but the opposition of doctrine and message does not come to grips with the issue and may do nothing but cause confusion. Theology is just as concerned with the "message" as is catechetics. Conversely, catechetics is at all times doctrinal, not only because human reflection leads to doctrinal understanding, but because even the most primitive "message" of Christianity is already a doctrinal formulation. The chief interest of both theology and catechetics is the revelation of God in Jesus Christ. This revelation is neither doctrine nor message, but is a real, personal intercommunion. When trying to convey some insight into this inexhaustible reality, both theology and catechetics use a doctrinally formulated message.

A sharp opposition of doctrine and message seems to be based on the assumption that the more primitive the formulation, the closer one is to the "pure" revelation. But the fact that one teaches the earliest apostolic discourses is no guarantee that one is conveying God's revelation in unadulterated simplicity, nor even that one is approaching more closely to it. Indeed, the attempt to avoid theological reflection upon the most primitive records of revelation does not succeed in getting rid of theology, but only in ingesting bad theology. Thus today there is building up in catechetical writing a new theological vocabulary not always supported by careful theological reflection. These new words are at first sight more personal and concrete, more "existential" and relevant, than the tired, old scholastic words. But the very reason why they are more immediately appealing is the same reason that they more quickly degenerate into jargon. What is needed to resolve this problem of terminology is not to create a new and still simpler vocabulary, but to stop hoping that the problem can be solved at this level and with these tools. What is needed today is not a further stripping away of theology, but more and better theology both in the preparation of religion teachers and in discussions concerning catechetical theory. Otherwise, with theology and catechetics removed from one another or sharply contrasted, catechetical writing turns in upon itself and ends by creating a new system of technical words—the very thing the catechetical movement set out to get rid of.

One catechetical writer, maintaining that the catechism should not be a summary of theology, goes on to say that "it is necessary to distinguish between knowledge concerning God and knowing God, intellectual assimilation and vital assimilation, doctrine and message, notional assent and real assent, a faith of principles and a faith of concrete realities, a faith that is simply knowledge of things of faith and faith as a way of salvation."[3] The question that must be raised with reference to such statements is not whether catechists are or should be in favor of the second set of aims as opposed to the first. The questions that must be asked are whether anyone prefers the first set over the second, whether this whole schema clarifies the relationship between theology and catechetics, and whether these contrasts are any help at all to teachers trying to understand their role in religious education. Obviously, catechists are more interested in the students knowing God than in knowing about God, but the serious questions are how catechists can make any contribution to the student coming to know God, and what the possibilities and limitations of any human being are in helping another to know God. A deep probing of these issues behind the new phrases is not always evident in catechetical writing. This, I would claim, is the great crisis of catechetics today: not the dying catechism and manual, but the still rising hope that the education of hundreds of millions of people in an incredibly complex world can be carried out with a bit of Scripture and liturgy and much sin-

---

[3] Fr. Marie, "El fin de la catequesis," in *Sinite,* II (1961), pp. 60–61.

cerity and good will. This simply is not enough. There is need for patient inquiry, deep understanding, and detailed knowledge.

It is often said in catechetical writing today: In the past we merely instructed the intellect in revealed truths; now we must concern ourselves with "forming the whole man." Some people may understand clearly what they mean to say with this formula, but some very dangerous ideas could easily lurk beneath the surface. Certainly, it is true that teaching "revealed truths" to the intellect of a child is insufficient (I would go further and say it is impossible). One must ask, however, whether the situation that practically everyone today revolts against has been understood, and more important still, whether the supposed remedies might not worsen the situation. It is very strange that catechetical writers keep saying that Catholic religion teaching has been too centered on knowledge and has neglected everything else. In actual fact, it would seem that religion books and religion teachers have never been wanting in exhortations to avoid sin, in imposing devotional and ascetical practices, in insisting upon frequent reception of sacraments, in maintaining strong external discipline, and so forth. The juxtaposition of these and numerous other things with the "holding of true doctrines" has never been lacking; and this is what constitutes a large part of our difficulty. The assumption that we have dealt too much with intellectual understanding and not enough with emotion is wrong on both counts.

On the one hand, we have never had in the teaching of religion too much concentration upon knowledge and understanding; we have had only too little of it. What has been most painfully lacking and what is most desperately needed is some intellectual seriousness and competence in the teaching of religion. It is preposterous to say that the ordinary catechism or theology manual is overly intellectual, too philosophical, excessively theological. "The fact that our textbooks are so little

35

alive, serve proclamation and witness so little, is not due to their superabundance of scholastic and scientific theology but because they offer too little of it."[4] In the teaching of religion our problem has not been in stopping at knowledge and understanding; would that we could get so far. We have not dealt exclusively with the intelligence of students precisely because the only way that their religious understanding could be reached would be through historical, bodily, and social experience.

On the other hand, if religion teaching has not succeeded in reaching the child's understanding, one must then ask where the real, operative, religious motivation has been coming from. The answer, it would seem, is that it has sprung from emotion, a distorted and dehumanized emotion because separated from understanding and freedom. In other words, while paying lip service to "intellect," religion teaching has usually been concerned with emotional reactions, particularly sentimentality and fear. We do not need more manipulation of children's emotions; we ought to have far less of it. While letting children experience their world, teaching ought to be directed to the intelligence of the children so that they may be freed from their fears. The constant refrain today about the need of less concern for intellectual learning in religion and more "training of the heart" not only misses what has been wrong in the past, but threatens to point us a hundred-eighty degrees in the wrong direction.

At the very moment when the Church stands in greatest need of an intellectual apostolate there is implicit in much catechetical writing a devaluation of intellectual understanding. Of course, it is always admitted and even strenuously asserted that the transmission of knowledge (the "revealed truths") is a necessary step along the way to forming Christians, but this shows an inadequate conception of the nature of Christian revelation. One must

[4] Karl Rahner, "The Prospects for Dogmatic Theology," in *Theological Investigations*, I, p. 7.

36

come to realize what it means to stand in the truth which sets men free. What is necessary is not something in addition to the "revealed truths" but a much deeper comprehension of Christian revelation. When this task is accomplished it will become apparent that the understanding of what it means to be a Christian is not a preliminary to be gotten through as an embarrassing preamble, but is itself the radical grasping hold of (or being grasped by) the Father of Truth.[5]

It has been said in recent years that what is needed to improve religious education is to place at its center the "core of the Gospel," the kerygma. This, it is said, will bring about "commitment." "The answer of the hearers is not always positive; it can be negative. What is not possible is indifference before the problem which the kerygma poses."[6] Unfortunately, however, indifference to what is posed by the kerygma is a cold, inescapable fact. Teachers find many students indifferent, uncomprehending, and uninterested in the whole thing. Other students who are not without interest seem incapable of making a choice for or against the Christian faith. Teachers and students alike are told that this new material is relevant to their lives, but nevertheless they find much of it foreign and unreal. They may find it more interesting than the old system (at least for a while), but it is still a *system*, a rigid construction of words and ideas imposed upon people from the outside to manipulate their lives.[7] Despite the talk

[5] Karl Rahner, "Über die Wahrhaftigkeit," in *Katechetische Blätter*, LXXXV (September, 1960), p. 414.

[6] Ignacio Mengs, "Pastoral, predicación, catequesis," in *Sinite*, IV (1963), p. 53.

[7] As I shall show in Chapter XI, some catechetical writers have moved on from the first enthusiastic "proclaimings of the message" to the deeper theological and anthropological questions that cannot long be avoided. The work of Alfonso Nebreda represents an important step forward. Besides his *Kerygma in Crisis*, one should also note his report on the Bangkok meeting that dealt with some of these further problems: "East Asian Study Week," in *Lumen Vitae*, XVII (December, 1962), pp. 717–730; it remains true, none-

about a concrete, personal revelation, it is still assumed that revelation is a report out of the past to be accepted by men of the present. The human person and his freedom remain outside of revelation; man's part is to respond to the things God offers. In this conception, faith is bound to be impersonal and separated from man's life. Faith will not be a response—if that word designates a free and conscious human act; faith instead will be coercion, if not by threat then by promise.

The overriding issue in our world today is *freedom*. This, it seems to me, is the *fact* from which discussion on religious education must begin. Catechetical writing even to the present seems almost completely blind to this fact. There is confidence that we have improved the "content of our message"; we know what is good for students and we can get them to respond to what we want them to do.[8] If catechetical writers wish to propose the "formation of the whole man," they must first face the fact that there is *no* direct way that one can accomplish the task. The whole man is the free man and his freedom must remain inviolate. A blunt, frontal attack upon a person's freedom with a mass of religious concepts and practices is bound by the nature of the case to fail. The difficult paradox in which the teacher finds himself is that the more he tries to form another's freedom, the more he diminishes what he is attempting to increase. I cannot form Christians; I cannot make men be free. As Kierkegaard among others has pointed out, the most that one can do for another is to try to help him by an indirect kind of

theless, that many new textbooks and much of the popular catechetical writing at present show a naïve optimism in constructing new systems out of biblical-liturgical data.

[8] The confident statement so often made that the catechetical movement has passed from an early methodological phase into the really important concentration on "content" shows the continuing failure to see the whole issue; Marcel van Caster has rightly criticized this dichotomy which should have been overcome; see his *The Structure of Catechetics* (New York, Herder and Herder, 1965), pp. 7–11.

communication to discover for himself the Christian he is called to be.[9]

We are so intent in catechetical presentations on converting the whole world that we refuse to admit the time, the patience, the effort, the indirectness necessary for such an undertaking. Our feeling today is: "Let us explain Christianity, all of it, immediately. If ten words do not suffice, let us have a hundred. We have no time in religion for anything but the right ideas, the correct words, the proper practices. With the latest in scientific exegesis, the most up-to-date liturgical practice, the new dynamic content in religion teaching, how can we fail?" The answer is that we can fail quite easily because the main issue is freedom.

Even on a purely psychological plane it is obvious that any appeal to freedom must be made in a far subtler and more indirect way than that apparent in religion textbooks and catechetical writing. What I am mainly concerned with, however, is the misunderstanding here of revelation. There is no real appreciation of the givenness of God's revelation in the Christian life and the need for the person to reflect freely upon that reality. There is still a narrowness in the conception of means at the teacher's disposal for helping students to do this. Catechists must be prepared to work for their ultimate goal in a far more indirect way than has often been supposed. They must be intent on awakening human beings to many things in their lives which have no immediate relation to a religious commitment but which are in fact the foundation on which a mature religious decision must be made today.[10] This, I hope to show, is not a tactical necessity forced upon us by the evils of the time, but is in accord with a theology of revelation.

The urgent question today is whether those who have worked

[9] See *The Point of View for My Work as an Author* (New York, Harper and Brothers, 1962), p. 41.

[10] See Josef Goldbrunner, "Catechesis and Encounter," in *New Catechetical Methods* (Notre Dame, University of Notre Dame Press, 1965), p. 34.

so hard to construct programs of religion teaching with carefully formulated patterns and vocabulary are willing to admit that all of this may be ineffectual and worthless unless they go to the student not only to speak but to listen. The oft-repeated principle that the role of the religion teacher is to "deliver the message" must be challenged. No *a priori* schema can be assumed to be the best material for educating young Christian students. The teaching material must largely be discovered in the common search by teacher and student, though the teacher should obviously contribute more because of his background of competence and experience. This orientation in religion teaching, I also hope to show, is not one of pragmatic adaptation to the breakdown of authority, but follows rather from the nature of Christian revelation itself.

These are a few of the problems and uncertainties that affect the catechetical movement today. In the following pages there is no pretension to work out a program to answer all the problems. Indeed, what is written above would indicate that there can be no such solutions. I do hope to clarify some working principles and to point toward areas which need further reflection and research. The theology of revelation cannot solve the catechetical problem, but the catechetical problem can become intelligible only through a continuing study of revelation. There is no room for resting on the improvements that have been made so far in the catechetical movement. This movement "is taking place through the action of the Holy Spirit in the life and thought of the Church. Giving great joy to those who participate to the full, it also gives a warning to those who persist in too partial a point of view."[11]

[11] Van Caster, *The Structure of Catechetics,* p. 11.

40

Part Two

IV.

Revelation, History, and Catechizing

In contemporary scriptural and theological writing on Christian revelation a concern for history has rapidly assumed a central role. The emphasis upon the historical character of revelation has found its way, at least as quickly and perhaps more ardently, into catechetical writing as well. Every teacher is being told these days that he must present revelation historically in order that his students may learn their "salvation history."[1]

If one asks the reason why history is so important in catechetical work, the immediate and obvious answer is that history was God's method of teaching and that man does better by imitating the means that God used rather than creating his own methods. "He took humanity as it was, like a child, teaching it what a child can grasp, and bringing it only by slow degrees to an understanding of greater mysteries. It is very important for us to meditate on this method of God's, because it will help us better to understand what our own missionary attitude should be."[2] This undoubtedly is the right direction for us to take, that

[1] See Derek Lance, *Teaching the History of Salvation* (Glen Rock, Paulist Press, 1964), pp. 27–56; *Directoire de pastorale catéchetique à l'usage des diocèses de France* (Paris, Editions Fleurus, 1964), p. 21, #21: "All catechesis should transmit its teaching in the perspective of the history of salvation. It should show how the events of this history have an ever present permanent meaning."

[2] Jean Daniélou, *The Salvation of the Nations* (Notre Dame, University of Notre Dame Press, 1962), p. 28.

43

is, we must meditate upon divine teaching in order better to understand our catechetical work. It must be understood, however, that we have here a starting point and not a conclusion. Not all questions are resolved by saying that God used history to teach and therefore we are to do the same. Teachers who wish to lead students into the "history of salvation" need to examine their own understanding of revelation and history lest they patch up old concepts with new words, and thus show that they fail to see the real significance of history in catechizing. Some of the casually repeated statements make one suspicious of how deep the understanding of "salvation history" is. The statement often made that God could have chosen many other ways to reveal himself but that he chose history as a good pedagogical tool is, if not false, at least theologically vapid.

While catechetical theorists exalt "salvation history" as the necessary answer to the way of presenting revelation, it does not take long to discover an undercurrent of opposition to this "approach" among many teachers of religion. To prevent an unfortunate dichotomy it is imperative that a deeper theological meaning of revelation in history be developed. Because many people have a superficial understanding of history to start with (what Collingwood calls the scissors-and-paste theory[3]), the confident announcements that revelation is history may confuse rather than clarify the issue. When attempts are made to take what is already a wrong conception of history and modify it according to the peculiar demands of exegetes, it may be a rather strange concoction that comes out as "salvation history."

When this elaborately conceived "salvation history" is transferred to the students, their conception of revelation is liable to be more artificial, contrived, and abstract than their non-historical notion ever was. Revelation may mean to them a collection of events in the remote past with interpretations supplied by some

[3] See *The Idea of History* (Oxford, Clarendon Press, 1946), pp. 274–282.

extraordinary men of the past, and all of this unrecognized except by a small group claiming to have a special perceptiveness. The enthusiastic claim of teachers and textbooks that "the revelation now presented to us in word goes back to an original revelatory event which did not occur exclusively in word but also . . . in the revelatory activity of God in history"[4] may not be particularly impressive to students of today. Nor is it obvious why it should be. The whole scheme of historical events will almost certainly be irrelevant to students if this body of recorded testimony is imposed from the outside as the truths and the precepts they must live by.

What must first be made clear is that the history we speak of in reference to Judaic-Christian revelation is not a collection of facts recorded in the past and handed down in books. Man is the being who makes history and history is man's self-understanding in time. Because history is not a collection of things outside man, because man is his history, then to say that God has entered history is to say that he enters into a personal relationship with man, that is, with every man in the structure of his real life situations. There is history in Christian revelation and there must always be history in catechizing not because God chose a good gimmick, but because God chose man. To learn of God's revelation means to discover God and man together, not an abstract humanity but the present person in the self-awareness of his own historical existence. Each person recommences with fundamental and unpredictable newness the dialogue with God. Just as the Jews of old discovered God in their historical experience, the Christian student of today can discover God only through the experience of his own situation of space, time, and community. The history in which God reveals himself is not only that of the

---

[4] Werner Bulst, *Revelation* (New York, Sheed and Ward, 1965), pp. 58–59.

Jewish people in the dim past, but that of the child in twentieth-century America.

The Old Testament record of revelation, as we shall later see, has a most important role to play in helping today's student to discover the revelation of God in his life. It remains true, nevertheless, that God enters the history of each man and that each man must find God in this present personal history if he is ever to find God. It is a fact that statements to this effect are very often made in catechetical literature today, but the statements are not taken literally nor pressed home. The main reason why they remain on the level of pious metaphors is an insufficient understanding of the nature of revelation, especially the doctrine of the "closing" of revelation. Catechetical writers are afraid to take seriously their own statements that God speaks to the student in the religion lesson. The result is that the student's own history is simply added to the scheme of past events or else the past is constantly "applied" to the present. The student's participation in the history, however, should not be tacked on at the end. It should rather be the starting point and the locus of all historical reflection.

The crucial question here is whether one is starting with real people and their real experience, elucidating that experience by an ever open and ever widening interpretation; or whether one begins with a set of truths that are self-interpretive and are imposed from the outside. And I would claim that a description of past events is—especially for a child—a set of propositional truths. A teacher with imagination can reconstruct a story from the past in a way that will catch the child's attention, but there is no way to make the events of some past life recorded in a story the facts of one's own life. The experience that Moses had of God may have been personal, concrete, and existential; but Moses is dead. That does not necessarily mean that what has been left by Moses or about Moses is irrelevant today. As a child begins to discover

46

himself in relation to others we would hope that a powerful means to understand his life will be found in what we know of Moses, Abraham, or Isaiah. But first the child has to be conscious, to feel, to think, to choose, to love and be loved.

Those who feel that history is simply a fad that is creating a new system for religion teaching are not without grounds for their complaints. "Salvation history" will not bring about a breakthrough from all depersonalizing systems unless there is clear recognition of the ever present danger of falling into new systems. There are not only scholastic systems; there are also biblical systems, liturgical systems, and historical systems. The mind of man is always ready to settle down into a comfortable system while still congratulating itself for having escaped from the old system of abstract truths. The creation of a tightly knit system of historical facts and interpretations would be no closer to meeting the real issues of the twentieth century and the real questions of growing Christians. Thus it is objected that "the insistence upon history, which to the theologian has seemed to be so attractive an apologetic, to the undecided layman and the world outside has continued to seem a somewhat irrelevant one."[5] In addition, it is said that a young person up to about the age of twelve has little sense of the historical past. The child thus finds it difficult to situate past events in relation to one another. The adolescent, though possessing a greater capability in this area, is often so dominated by his present situation that he cares little for past events.[6]

These objections should be taken into account by anyone advocating the teaching of "salvation history." If young people are

[5] James Barr, "Revelation through History in the Old Testament and in Modern Theology," in *New Theology No. 1*, edited by Martin E. Marty and Dean G. Peerman (New York, Macmillan, 1964), p. 72.

[6] See Xavier La Bonnardière, *Devoir de croire et sincerité intellectuelle* (Paris, Aubier, 1949), pp. 153–158; see also Pierre Babin, *Crisis of Faith* (New York, Herder and Herder, 1963), pp. 53–54.

generally incapable of doing critical historical study of the past and if they are limited in their ability to see the great sweep of past history, it would be unwise to overload their minds with copious materials from historical studies. On the other hand, I maintain that a theology of revelation demands that the history which the teaching of revelation begins with is always the student's own history. The student will not adequately understand this history until he eventually comes to see it within the cosmic history of God's relation with the Jewish people, the humanity of Jesus, the members of the Church, and the entire community of mankind. Nevertheless, it is only by working from his own experience, that is, from the revelational history which constitutes his life, that he will come to grasp this whole plan. He cannot be attentive to the history of the world until he is attentive to the things and people around himself. What he first needs is an awakening to his own world of events and people, an awakening to the wonders of everything in the universe.

Judaic-Christian revelation is not "natural religion"; we believe that the natural and the human must be transformed and transcended. As the Jews of the Old Testament were invited to leave pagan idols and enter into a relationship with the true God, so the student of today is invited to go beyond all natural religion. The human cannot be transcended, however, unless it is accepted in the process. If faith is based upon the negativities of human existence, then God will be inserted through the crevices and made the answer to some problem of the moment instead of being understood as the presupposition and end of all history. Only by accepting the historical and human as the locus of God's revealing activity can the God of Christians, the Lord of history, be found. Undoubtedly, there is some danger here of reducing Christian faith and revelation to a secularized humanism, and it is a danger never lightly to be dismissed. Paradoxically, however, the danger of turning Christianity into a self-enclosed

48

secularism is greatest precisely where the historical process is opposed in the name of faith. Those who try to escape from history and to prevent historical development in Christianity end not by choosing God over man, but by idolizing the elements of a past culture.

The acceptance of history as revelatory means the recognition and appreciation of human personality as the openness to God. There can be no revelation unless a human person is being discovered in relationship to God and the human community. Christian revelation is not a veneer to hide the raw material of personality, not a collection of bandages and potions with which to patch up a sinful humanity. It must be the perfection of what is truly human. The discovery and acceptance of the human is neither easy nor inevitable. It is just as possible and just as frequent for men to escape from history today as it was in primitive times.[7] It is just as important as ever that today's student face his own historical situation and his own community. This acceptance of his own personal history is not only the presupposition of revelation, it is in some way the revelation itself. "Everything that detaches the child and man from himself, which opens windows on reality, nature, his fellows, has a religious significance."[8]

What was also true of the Old Testament people in their historical development is true of the young person growing up today: there is an incapacity to commit oneself totally from the beginning. Situations must be experienced, assimilated, and

---

[7] See Mircea Eliade, *Cosmos and History* (New York, Harper Torchbooks, 1959), p. 111: "Neither in Christianity nor in Judaism does the discovery of this new dimension in religious experience, faith, produce a basic modification of traditional conceptions. Faith is merely made possible for each individual Christian. The great majority of so-called Christian populations continue, down to our day, to preserve themselves from history by ignoring it and by tolerating it rather than by giving it the meaning of a negative or positive theophany."

[8] Piet Fransen, "Toward a Psychology of Divine Grace," in *Research in Religious Psychology* (Brussels, Lumen Vitae, 1957), p. 19.

pondered. Man must grow up according to the rhythm that belongs to human life. A fully human and moral decision, as Newman showed, is always the result of a personally experienced history.[9] It would be illusory and harmful to deny the necessity of this process of growth which cannot be hurried over by impatient teachers. Instead of trying to push students beyond what they are capable of sustaining at a particular stage, the teacher ought to cooperate with the rhythm of time that God gives to man to progress toward maturity. It is by accepting this natural growth that the strength and impetus will be found to go beyond it.[10]

The general awareness of human growth and development, however, is not enough. It is not only humanity that must be affirmed, it is not just an abstract human nature with its powers that must be accepted as good. God reveals himself in the concrete history of the person, and it is this individual person with his whole past, present, and future that the catechist must accept and work with. God began with the Israelites where they were, in all of their weakness, deformity, and sinfulness. Their repeated failures did not cut them off from God, but instead gave occasion to God's continuing acts of love. Their past was not denied or destroyed; on the contrary, God continually made use of their past to teach them.

Every catechist who hopes to aid a student in taking up a revelatory relationship with God must realize the fact that there

[9] See *A Grammar of Assent* (Garden City, Doubleday Image Book, 1955), p. 85: "Even when that assent is not the result of concurrent causes, if such a case is possible, . . . still its presence argues a special history, and a personal formation, which an abstraction does not. For an abstraction can be made at will, and may be the work of a moment; but the moral experiences which perpetuate themselves in images, must be sought after in order to be found, and encouraged and cultivated in order to be appropriated."

[10] See Josef Goldbrunner, *Cure of Mind and Cure of Soul* (2nd edition; New York, Pantheon, 1958), pp. 103–120; Pierre-André Liégé, *Consider Christian Maturity* (Chicago, Priory Press, 1965), p. 29.

is a history of mankind sedimented in the individual. Even further, there exists for the individual at every stage of development a concrete, personal, experienced history that cannot be revoked. The present moment of the person can be faced only if the past and future have been accepted. Any attempt to separate a student from his past by negating its existence cannot succeed. An "overcoming" of the past can take place only by accepting the past in the light of a promise for the future. A catechist who refuses to work with the actual history of the student's life cannot be much of a help in mediating God's revelation. The teacher who would refuse to recognize that the student (especially one from poor social conditions) must be attracted to God and not simply made to obey is hardly acting as an ambassador of Christ.[11]

There must be a gradual growth into the Christian life with no shock when failure occurs and with no pretense that unlimited possibilities exist at any moment. Just as with the Israelites, it is often a laborious struggle but one in which the context of interpretation continually widens. Every choice for the truth of God opens unsuspected possibilities for the future. The best preparation that the student can make for the future is the living of a revelational life in the present and an understanding of this life as far as he can manage to grasp it.[12] The education he receives in the present must be meaningful in the here and now and must at the same time avoid setting up barriers to future development. Every genuinely Christian teaching will be directed to the present person, using the past and opening to the future. The student cannot be taught all that he will need for living and defending his faith, but he must acquire an interest

[11] See F. H. Drinkwater, *Telling the Good News* (London, Macmillan, 1960), p. 162.
[12] See Henri Oster, "God's Plan," in *Readings in European Catechetics,* edited by George Delcuve and André Godin (Brussels, Lumen Vitae, 1962), pp. 50–51.

in and a love of learning that will enable him to learn whatever has to be learned later in life.

The catechist, like the prophet of Israel, is always in the position of helping people to free themselves from the childish idols which detain their full acceptance of a vocation from God and man. The catechist must gently urge them forward, believing in them and desiring the full development of their human potentialities. The catechist must help them to see the significance of the episodes that make up their histories. The full significance of the events in their lives cannot be immediately seen, and for this reason the students' history must be written afresh every year.

As was true in Israelite history, the student of today is continually faced with the temptation to turn aside and look for an easier path. Despite the love of God that is poured out to them and despite the encouraging words of the catechist, many students will turn back upon themselves and refuse to go forward to a Christian vocation. What the catechist needs in viewing this historical struggle of emerging youth is the basic virtue of the Israelite prophet: hope. To hope is to look on the child with the eyes of God. God is he who sees man in all the unrealized potentialities of his being. A catechist is never justified in saying that such and such a case is hopeless. Man is not in a position to make such a judgment. In addition, the judgment itself may have very harmful effects. To hope in another is to help the other to create himself in the realization of his possibilities. To despair of another is in some way to stifle this process and to destroy.[13]

As to whether modern man is generally concerned with and greatly responsive to the workings of history and the study of history, we meet here with a fundamental ambivalence. It is often assumed that history is the dominating characteristic of

[13] See Gabriel Moran, "Hope: Foundation of Religious Education," in *Catholic Educational Review*, LXI (May, 1963), pp. 302–312; see also Gabriel Marcel, "Sketch of a Phenomenology and a Metaphysic of Hope," in *Homo Viator* (New York, Harper Torchbook, 1962), pp. 49–50.

modern times, especially since Hegel. A passion for the discovery
of precise facts about the distant past combined with an evolu-
tionary sense supported by both biology and technology give the
impression of a keen historical sense. Man's interests and his
vision are today without limits in any direction. History is no
longer based upon select documents of the past; now, as Collingwood has said, "everything in the world is potential evidence for
any subject whatever."[14]

The one gnawing weakness in this modern vision of history
is that with a rejection of Christian faith it has no ultimate basis,
neither beginning, nor end, nor reason for the whole. Judaic-
Christian revelation did not teach men how to use modern tools
of research, but it did provide the inspiration for accepting human history and seeing a meaning in it. If this meaning is removed and if history has no support from beyond itself, all the
technical improvements within the process may instead of freeing man succeed only in creating a more efficient slavery. Technical progress separated from both religious faith and humanistic
consideration tends to be mistaken for history, whereas it is only
movement staggered by dates. It is concerned less with human
history and more with physico-economic time.[15]

The teaching on Christian revelation, therefore, must be united
with humanistic study and scientific technology in reciprocally
illuminating relationships. Separated from one another, these can
only result on the one hand in an abstractly conceived "sacred
history" which is almost totally irrelevant to modern man, and
on the other hand in an exaggerated optimism or pessimism
about man's possibilities for the future. But a sacred history that
would really emerge out of the Christian life in the contemporary world would be far from outdated or irrelevant. In fact,

14 *Op. cit.*, p. 280.
15 Albert-Marie Besnard, "Is Our Technical Civilization Open to the
Gospel?," in *Lumen Vitae*, XIII (1958), pp. 607–609.

as Karl Rahner has observed, "it is really only now that Christianity is beginning to have its true opportunity. For what Christianity, as the religion of all men, has always been looking for—one single world with one united history—is only now beginning to exist."[16] To modern man, historical man, man who has discovered freedom and personal dignity, Christian revelation has an ultimate word to speak.

There is then no question of choosing a contemporary fad or gimmick, there is no question of "making use" of history to teach revelation. The one question at issue is whether God is someone real who reveals himself in the real life history of men. The astonishing charge against Christianity that it destroys man's historical sense has grounds to the extent that revelation is conceived of merely as truths from the past being applied to the present. The contemporary emphasis upon the events of Israelite history does not overcome this difficulty. This emphasis upon events will be a help only if the events of Christian time are taken in all seriousness to be revelatory of God. Christians believe that God has taken man into a definitive relationship in Christ. It is in Christ and his brothers that the definitive revelation now happens.

The Christian is the one who is called to see the truth of his own historical life and that of the community's in relation to God. The Christian must be given help to face the real-life situations of his personal history and by accepting them to find God in that history as part of the whole history of man's life with God. The events which the teacher must be especially attentive to are the events which make up the student's life as these events can be understood through other persons and most especially through the unique person, Jesus Christ.

[16] See "The Scholar," in *Theology for Renewal,* p. 88.

54

V.

Christ as the Center

In the last chapter we have considered the place of the student's history as it is understood through the total history of God's dealing with man. This history cannot be taught apart from its culmination and recapitulation in Jesus Christ. A reflection upon the student's life will always be, at least implicitly, a reflection upon the one who realized personal existence to the full. The presentation of Christian revelation thus finds its starting point in the relationship of the present Christian community to Christ. From there the perspective can be broadened to include God's revelatory relationship with the people who led up to Christ.[1]

If Jesus is the fullness of revelation and the center of our religion, then it is through an intimacy with him that all other things in the Christian life are to be understood. Children should learn of him without first having to go through a multiplicity of doctrines on Adam and Eve, original sin, angels and devils.[2] First the students must come to know Christ; then these doctrines will be illumined by his person. The figure of Christ does

---

[1] See St. Augustine, *The First Catechetical Instruction* ("Ancient Christian Fathers"; Westminster, Newman, 1946), pp. 83–84.

[2] See Georg Hansemann, "Zugänge und Schwierigkeiten bezüglich der Christusverkündigung beim Schulkind der Gegenwart," in *Die Christusverkündigung in der Schule* (Graz Wien Köln, Verlag Styria, 1963), pp. 57–58; Klemens Tilmann, "Bible, Source of Christian Doctrine," in *Lumen Vitae,* XII (September, 1956), p. 609.

emerge, of course, from its Jewish ancestry, and for that reason some antecedent familiarity with the Old Testament will be a necessary element in understanding him. But the significance of Christ's life breaks out of the shell of its own prophetic preparation and sheds light upon all history. Israel had represented all the nations when she spoke; now Christ speaks all that was best in Israelite tradition and broadens her concept of neighbor to include all men. Everything in reality had flowed toward the meeting of God and man until God finally spoke from within the flesh of a human nature. In the happening of the Christ, light and direction was given to all those who were ready to learn. The world complains that the concept of God is empty and Christianity can only agree; but it adds that God himself has filled in the meaning, that is, he has defined himself through a life, death, and resurrection.

Jesus Christ was God revealing, but he was also God veiled. Not all who came into contact with him in his historical life recognized who he was. Not all who have some knowledge of him today know who he is. "He appeared open to those who sought Him with all their hearts and hidden to those who fled Him with all their hearts. There was light enough for those whose only desire was to see Him, darkness enough for those who wanted it otherwise."[3] No doubt this is true, but for many people today, both Christian and non-Christian, child and adult, he is not so much rejected as unknown. The name of Christ is constantly used and various doctrines are propagated in his name. Often, however, there is little attention given to the process of growth involved in coming to know any person. Many minds are not attuned in our day to the knowledge of friendship. The human atmosphere in which one person can answer to another must be prepared if Jesus Christ is to be a real person for stu-

[3] Brother Philippe André, "Christ's Pedagogy in the Gospels," in *Modern Catechetics*, p. 339.

dents. When there is no preparing of the ground and when all that concerns him is not taken seriously and reverently, then all the words poured out about him not only fail to bring about a knowledge of him, but they also deaden the possibility of this occurring in the future. "Thus he remains a stranger to them: they know much about him but they do not know him; they have learned of him but they have not met him; they listen to his word but they do not hear it—and therefore can give no real and effective response."[4] It is not more words that are needed but the right words, those that emerge from a Christian community that has a deep appreciation of the person of Christ.

When there has been generated some interest, or at the very least curiosity, in regard to this strange and awesome figure of Christ, then the written testimony which Christianity possesses can function with some effectiveness. In that testimony every word, gesture, attitude, and action of Christ has indefinite depths of meaning for true inquirers. Provided that the gospel is not reduced to a source book of "revealed truths," it will be a continuing help for the child, adolescent, and adult. The extraordinary works of Jesus will be taken not as external criteria for his mission nor illustrations of his doctrines, but as religious symbols that allow us some entrance into the knowledge of God.[5] If you want to know what God is like, Christianity claims, then meditate on the words and works of the one called Christ.

In Jesus Christ, God gives himself to the world, the Father's love is revealed to the world, and man's relation to the Father through Son and Spirit is revealed. There is no reason why the doctrine of the Trinity and man's relation to the Trinity cannot be implicit from the start of Christian teaching. This would be an improvement over the attempt to attach the doctrine of the

[4] Hansemann, "Zugänge und Schwierigkeiten bezüglich der Christusverkündigung beim Schulkind der Gegenwart," *loc. cit.*, p. 48.
[5] See Roger Mace, "Les miracles de l'Evangile dans l'enseignement religieux," in *Catéchistes*, LIII (January, 1963), p. 65.

Trinity to an original monotheism. The New Testament does not say simply that Christ is God;[6] Jesus never presented himself as an oracle of truths that were to be written down and learned by men. He did present himself as the one who is sent by the Father and the one who invites men to share in a communion with him in returning to the Father. The Trinity is not one doctrine among many taught in Christian revelation; rather, Christian revelation is of its nature Trinitarian. No worse indictment of religious education could be made than the fact that few Catholics would think of the doctrine of the Trinity as the central and controlling belief of their lives.[7]

Christian revelation, therefore, is especially the revelation of Father, Son, and Spirit, or else it can hardly be called Christian. Christ reveals the fatherhood of God and the way of divine love that leads to the Father. It is not so much by long explanations about the Father but by Christ's presence among men and his prayerful communion with the Father that he reveals the whole plan of God's love. It is that kind of presence and union that is prerequisite to making the doctrine of the Trinity intelligible. If there is true Christian brotherhood and responsible use of authority in the teaching of religion and in the whole community, then the revelation of the Trinity will take on meaning. Where

[6] On the catechetical and liturgical significance of the New Testament use of the word "God" with reference to Christ, see Karl Rahner, "Theos in the New Testament," in *Theological Investigations,* I, pp. 143–148; Raymond E. Brown, "Does the New Testament Call Jesus God?," in *Theological Studies,* XXVI (December, 1965), pp. 545–573.

[7] See Mary Perkins Ryan, "The Christian and the Trinity," in *Twenty-Fifth North American Liturgical Week. The Challenge of the Council: Person, Parish, World,* XXV (1964), p. 228: "My husband was once discussing the whys and wherefores of Catholic education with a group of distinguished Catholic educators, and he remarked that the real test of a Catholic education was whether a graduate was aware of how his belief in the Trinity should affect the way he acted on a crowded bus. The distinguished educators looked at one another in an embarrassed kind of way and admitted that they themselves didn't know the answer."

these are absent the Trinity can mean little more than a puzzle of words.

In the figure of Jesus Christ, God should speak to students. This can hardly occur, however, unless Jesus is clearly understood to be man. At first glance, it may seem that the humanity of Christ is appreciated, even overstressed in Christian piety. In actual fact, however, despite the pictures and stories, prayers and devotions, Bethlehem and Calvary imagery, it is difficult to find the *man*. There is more often a sentimental piety of "God dying for us" with little appreciation of the fact that humanity in the ultimate depths of its receptive power is lived out in the human life of Jesus. It is not quite accurate, however, to say that we have overstressed Christ's divinity and we must restore the balance by stressing his humanity more. A balance would be a relatively easy thing to attain, but it would be useless and dangerous; for Christian belief is directed not to a being half-god and half-man, but to one truly God and truly man. We do not really have a choice here; we cannot emphasize humanity or divinity in Christ; we find both or we have found neither. It is only in the "this-worldly" God that the Transcendent appears; it is only when Christ is understood as the culmination of the human that we discover the incomprehensible God dwelling among us. If students have little appreciation of Christ's humanity, then very likely they do not think of him as God either. "It is sometimes a kind of useless, denatured Docetism they subscribe to. They do not picture Christ as fully human, but neither do they think of him as fully divine. . . . Their real assent is to Christ as a kind of superman or demi-God."[8] The drive in contemporary theology, therefore, to reaffirm the real manhood of Jesus is not for the sake of diminishing our appreciation of God's power, transcendence, and otherness. On the contrary, God will be God

[8] Paul Hilsdale, "Superman versus Christ — God versus Demi-God," in *Living Light*, I (Winter, 1965), p. 19.

for us only when we see his glory as manifested in the face of Christ Jesus (2 Cor. 4:6).

What sharply distinguishes Christianity from all ancient myth is not a belief that God appeared on earth to deliver truths from on high. What Christians believe is that the Word became flesh so that man no longer stands alone before God. In Christ man reaches full awareness of himself, his destiny, and his undreamed of capacity to be taken up into the life of God. All of man's introspection could never have brought him to see what human life is revealed to be when it is seen as the life of the Son of God. The recognition of Christ as man ought to be the revelation of the depth and beauty of all that is human. Conversely, all that is human and beautiful can be seen to lead to the one who lives human life to the full. He did not come distributing solutions to problems, but he came and lived human life to the end. He cannot be inserted into human life by pious phrases, but he can be found in a humanity opening beyond itself to the God who loves the world he has fashioned.

The humanity of Christ, therefore, will not become real to students simply by insistence upon the formula of Chalcedon. It is necessary to take seriously what is written in the gospel. For this reason, New Testament scholarship is an indispensable aid for teachers of religion because it is through such study that the development in the life of Jesus can be traced. Exegesis has made great advances in this area. Unfortunately, the theological studies of revelation have yet to incorporate this most central aspect of revelation, namely, its reception and development in the consciousness and freedom of the man Jesus.[9] As a result, one would suspect that there has been little change in the conception of

[9] In *Theology of Revelation* I have criticized the two recent theologies of revelation by Latourelle and Bulst on this point. Other Catholic theologians, however, have begun to bring out the receptiveness and the human development of Christ; see the references to Rahner, Schillebeeckx, Mersch, Urs von Balthasar, Mouroux, Galot, Congar.

revelation by saying that "Christ is the revelation." Revelation is still assumed to be *something* delivered to man, if not by statements from the heavens, then by the statements and actions of a divine messenger. The catechetical consequences of this continuing theological inadequacy are particularly distressing.

Human life means history and the human life of Jesus, if it is to be taken seriously by students must be seen as one of real, historical development. Jesus advanced in wisdom, age, and favor before God and man (Lk. 2:52). His human psychology was affected by the influence of Mary and Joseph and the social conditions of his time. His way of thinking and his modes of expression reflect his milieu and the past history of his people.[10] He is not some abstract universal norm of human nature. Instead, he became the norm, the supreme example of human life, by living a single, concrete history. He does not command his young followers to do more than is possible and appropriate for their particular age and development. Liégé notes that in contrast to the apocryphal writings, the authentic gospels do not advance the adult decisions of Christ's life into his childhood.[11] It would be well if the religious education of students followed the gospels scrupulously on this point.

Confident that the will of God was neither arbitrary nor absurd, Christ followed the will of his Father in obedience unto death. He contrasted his own attitude of patient endurance to that of unbelievers and to that of his own relatives (Jn. 7:6–8). He refused to escape from time, but waited instead for the hour that would be his. Christian students ought to be presented this life in a way that might awaken the realization that man can do no better than follow this path of patient acceptance. They

[10] See Jean Galot, "Science et conscience de Jésus," in *Nouvelle revue théologique,* LXXXII (February, 1960), p. 129; Yves Congar, *Jesus Christ* (New York, Herder and Herder, 1966), pp. 53–56.
[11] See *Consider Christian Maturity,* p. 30.

are not to clutch for a security to fall back upon, nor worry over past failures, nor be frightened by future suffering, but they are to live with confidence in the present. They will find if they do so that they are not alone in this long and often painful struggle of time and growth. "In every Christian, Christ relives his life anew: first as a child, then as a mature and responsible adult. He lives and grows in each of us, that our faith may increase, our love may be strengthened, our Christianity constantly deepened."[12]

For all of this to happen, however, it is important that the Christ who relives his life in Christians be presented as he is today. We cannot know him unless we know his past, but it is also true that we do not really know him unless we know him living, revealing, and sanctifying in his glorious person today. Nothing would seem to be more obvious, and yet the piety presented to young Christians has often manifested a startling incongruity. "There is no Baby Jesus *now*. There is only the glorious and immortal God-man Jesus Christ, who has conquered sin and death and is the living head of the Church His body."[13] The God whom the student is called to meet is God giving himself to man in the revelatory-redemptive communion of the risen Lord. All Christian teaching and exhortation ought to leave no ambiguity on this point.

It is not wholly adequate to speak of a "Christ event" in the past as the end of revelation. The only revelation that can conquer time is not an event but a continuing personal communion. No recollection of his words, no biblical hermeneutic, would of itself be sufficient to explain the continued actuality of God's

[12] Romano Guardini, *The Lord* (Chicago, Henry Regnery Co., 1954), pp. 451–452.

[13] Sister Maria de la Cruz Aymes-Coucke, "Teaching the Very Young 'in Spirit and in Truth': Kindergarten, First and Second Grade," in *Modern Catechetics*, p. 120.

revealing himself in Christ.[14] Only if Jesus has reached the perfection of his revelatory-redemptive activity to be continuously present among men taking part in revelation with them do we have a basis for the student's experience of Christian revelation in the present. Since the student is to live now, to worship now, to be sanctified now, he must know God revealing himself now, and not a God who retired from the world leaving his truths behind him.

If the death-resurrection of Jesus Christ is not the first of religious facts to be taught to the Christian student, it should still be the central and dominant fact. It may be that the student cannot appreciate the significance of this fact at the beginning of his religious education, but it must be implicit from the start. The death-resurrection as the act which recapitulates Christ's history must be for the Christian the center of world history. In that action, God gives us the justifying and judgmental act that obliges us to make a decision on the course of our destiny. Every other fact will assume importance according to its proximity to this center of revelation, for the resurrection is not one event among many in the past, but the beginning of a new life that continues in the present. The resurrection of Jesus is the definitive and irrevocable pledge of man's destiny, the first installment of his inheritance. "The importance of the new emphasis on the risen Christ is not just that this element of revelation will receive new stress; this emphasis creates a whole new context or atmosphere for the communication of Christian faith. It creates a sense of immediacy, a sense of reality; it pre-

[14] See Myles Bourke, "The Eucharist in the Church," in *Twenty-Fifth North American Liturgical Week. The Challenge of the Council: Person, Parish, World,* XXV (1964), pp. 38–39; see also Edward Schillebeeckx, *Christ the Sacrament of the Encounter with God* (New York, Sheed and Ward, 1963), pp. 40–45; F. X. Durrwell, *The Resurrection* (New York, Sheed and Ward, 1960), pp. 209–227.

pares for the impact which comes through direct encounter with the Person of Christ."[15]

The passage of Christ to the Spirit ought not to be presented as a loss to mankind. Having conquered sin and death, he is able to manifest in his nature liberty and joy, availability and transparency. Transfigured in glory, he has become free for mankind, not the men of Palestine of the year thirty, but free for all men of all time.[16] The passage of Christ beyond the world of corruption is the guarantee that man is not lost in a universe of staggering size and distances. The triumph of the love of God over man's anxiety before death is uttered for all time in the resurrection of Christ. He is God's "Amen," in him the promises of God found their "Yes." (See 2 Cor. 1:19–20; Apoc. 3:14.)

Christianity's great argument, her one great sign inviting men to believe is Christ and his Church. He shows his power and love most clearly and wins over children and adults most strikingly when he is manifested in the lives of his followers. They are the present sign of the resurrection as they gaze upon the whole world transformed by his redeeming love. If Christ's resurrection is not evident in the lives of his followers, no other sign can be very convincing to people. This is especially true for the adolescent, who looks for the sign of the resurrection in the joy and in the passion for justice which ought to characterize Christian lives. "The event which young people seek and which they await is always the same: the Easter Event. It is not enough for them to read in the Gospel that Jesus Christ came out of the tomb one day, 2,000 years ago. They must witness, here and

[15] Cooke, "Theology and Catechetical Renewal," *loc. cit.,* p. 90; see also François Coudreau, "The Place of the Paschal Mystery in Teaching the Catholic Faith," in *Living Light,* I (Winter, 1965), pp. 72–81.

[16] Charles Moeller, "Is It Possible, in the Twentieth Century, to Be a Man of the Bible?," in *Liturgy and the Word of God* (Collegeville, Liturgical Press, 1959), p. 154; see also Jean Mouroux, "Connaître Jésus-Christ," in *Catéchèse,* II (January, 1962), pp. 409–424.

now, a beginning of the resurrection of the flesh, in the paths of grace and hope."[17]

The continuing role of Christ in the revelation-redemption means that God's gift to the world in Christ is a reality of the future as well as of the present and past. The Church is always looking forward to the final, glorious manifestation of her Lord when the building up of the body will be complete.[18] There is an amazing attractiveness to young people today in this cosmic Christological teaching, the vision of a still developing reality. This is strong testimony to the fact of the power of Christ's revelation when it is seen in the broader perspective of human and world history and in the community of persons who profess their faith in a present and future Lord.[19]

[17] Babin, *Crisis of Faith*, p. 182.
[18] See *Constitution on Divine Revelation*, Chapter I, Article 4.
[19] See Jean Honore, "Les trois types de catéchèse christologique," in *Catéchèse*, II (October, 1962), pp. 425–440.

VI.

Apostles, Teachers, and Students

IN the Christian notion of revelation as I have presented it, the apostles occupy an indispensable role in the foundation of the Church.[1] They are not the receivers of "revealed truths" to be written down and studied in the later Church, but they are the ones through whom all revelation does come to the Church. Theirs was the unique experience of Jesus Christ in whom revelation reached its fullness. Contrary to what is usually implied, the main recipient of the revelation was not the apostolic community but Christ. The apostles do not ask us to accept *their message;* they invite us to share in a belief that goes beyond either of us.[2] I suggest that a reflection upon this role of apostle in the revelational process might be helpful in understanding the role of the catechist and the possibilities and limitations of his work.

The catechist cannot claim to be another apostle in the sense in which the word is used of the original witnesses. He can and must strive to share in the knowledge of Christ that the apostles had. The Father sent the Son and the Son sent men to found a

---

[1] See Moran, *Theology of Revelation,* pp. 77–94; see also Jean Levie, "Le message de Jésus dans la pensée des apôtres," in *Nouvelle revue théologique,* LXXXIII (January, 1961), pp. 25–49.

[2] See Karl Hermann Schelkle, *Discipleship and Priesthood* (New York, Herder and Herder, 1965), p. 31.

Church in his name. All of the members of that Church, insofar as they partake of the same vision that the apostles had, are also impelled to share their experience with others. The catechist, like the apostle, presents his life and teaching as a testimony to some reality beyond himself. "The apostles speak in concepts and preach a doctrine, but what they are bringing into the world is a presence. They are themselves sacraments of the presence of the dead and risen Christ."[3]

If students never recognize an actual, personal call coming from religion teaching, there is likely something wrong with the catechizing. Nevertheless, it is not the catechist's prerogative to demand recognition and acceptance of the divine invitation. The Spirit works where he wills and how he wills and it is not for man to control him. The catechist, like the apostle, invites men to respond to God, but when, where, and under what conditions is not for the catechist to decide. What the catechist can do is show what a Christian life is by living one. Furthermore, he can approach the student at the level of human revelation. This means that he offers the possibility of a personal relationship which may begin to awaken realization of the deeper, already existing revelatory relationship with God. The building of personal relationships and the intimacy of shared experience are the basis for a reflexive understanding of God's revelation. Before religious instruction begins there can and must be a vital assimilation going on, a true learning process, and a movement toward the Father.

There is no need to fear for the objective elements which have a legitimate place in Christian revelation. These must not be excluded, but neither should they be emphasized at the beginning of religious education.[4] From the start, Christianity should

---

3 Durrwell, *The Resurrection*, p. 310.

4 See Marie Fargues, *Catéchisme pour notre temps* (Paris, Editions Spes, 1951), p. 33; see also Jean Mouroux, *From Baptism to the Act of Faith* (Boston, Allyn and Bacon, 1964), p. 56.

be presented as primarily a question of people rather than things, an interpersonal communion of God and the community. Given such a context, a growth in appreciation could conceivably replace the boredom of covering the same old things which were exhausted long ago. Implementing this principle does not mean that the catechist keeps repeating that Jesus Christ is a person or keeps saying that God is someone who speaks to them. What it means first and indispensably is that the catechist must have a personal attitude and act with the respect and love for every person that Jesus Christ demands of his followers.

As the apostles were established in the fullness of revelation by the gift of the Holy Spirit, so too the catechist and the child stand in revelatory relationship to God and in sympathy toward one another by reason of that same Spirit. This sympathy gives the catechist the hope of evoking by his words the student's consciousness of his faith and vocation. What they are in Christ gives testimony to what is said to them in Christ. The gift of the Spirit means that there is a directive action of Christ within each man. This centrality of the Spirit is to be distinguished from a common conception which pays much lip service to the Spirit of God, but actually reduces him to an x-factor that fills in the gaps after the catechist finishes. The formula is not instruction plus Spirit equals formation, but instruction "in the Spirit"—which does not magically lead anywhere but which may contribute to the eventual emergence of an adult believer.[5]

The center of revelation, I have repeatedly affirmed, is the conscious experience that Christ had of the Father. The catechist must not look to St. John or St. Paul as the end, but must follow them in looking beyond themselves to Christ who receives from the Father. There can be a great flexibility of approach in trying

[5] See Edward Farley, "Does Christian Education Need the Holy Spirit? II: The Work of the Spirit in Christian Education," in *Religious Education*, LX (November, 1965), p. 430.

to enter this God-man relationship. The New Testament admits of various formulations for the announcement of Jesus as Lord simply because it is not the collection of individual facts that is most important, but the one to whom these and many other facts point.[6] Indeed, once Christ is understood to be the high point of human existence, everything becomes a pointer to him. Everything that arouses admiration for this person can find a place in the catechetical presentation of revelation. On the other hand, a proliferation of details and a drawing out of doctrines must not be forced upon children, inquirers, or converts. The prior experience must always be strong enough to sustain such development.

The teacher, like the apostle, is minister to the Word of God, but the Word is a person who cannot be understood by verbal explanations alone. The Word cannot be possessed, controlled, and used by the catechist for his purposes. The personal Word of God and his scriptural word in the Church stand over against the catechist in such a way as never to be dominated or manipulated. The catechist is to serve the Word and through service and experience point to this Word in his teaching.

What was true of the apostolic experience is true for both catechist and catechized, namely, that a pre-predicative, experienced relationship is the indispensable foundation of Christian revelation. In insisting upon the importance of such religious experience, however, I do not mean to deny or to underestimate the role of intellectual understanding. Precisely the contrary is true. It is through such deep religious experience that understanding is reached. There should be no question of a choice between them and any claim to have one without the other would have to be considered highly suspect.[7]

This returns me to a point touched upon in the first part of

6 See Dodd, *Apostolic Preaching,* p. 74.
7 See Roger Aubert, *Le problème de l'acte de foi* (3rd edition; Louvain, E. Waring, 1958), p. 715.

this study, that is, revelation as a knowledge relationship. I have pointed out the fact that recent catechetical literature has given the impression of lessening the role of knowledge in favor of other elements to be added to doctrinal teaching. The trouble with speaking of the "mere acquisition of knowledge" is that this assumes that Christian knowledge is quite easy to acquire, that it can be gotten as a preliminary and be generally finished with before one sets out on the road to living a Christian life.

Christ told his apostles that the truth would set them free. But it was only with a lifetime of struggle that the apostles— and Christ himself—achieved the perfection of truth. Christ did not bestow upon his apostles a knowledge of "revealed truths" to which he then added other elements. Instead, he began his apostles on their way to the knowledge and understanding of Christian revelation. Similarly, in Christianity today the knowledge and understanding is not so much at the beginning as at the end. Catechists ought not to transmit knowledge and then proceed to "form" Christians. Their role is to set students on the road toward understanding by helping them to use their intelligences creatively, originally, and constructively. If some taste for Christian learning, some sense of inquiry and discovery were conveyed in the schools, people might discover through a lifelong learning process what it means to be a Christian. It is here that formal teaching has its role to play, and it ought to take its own apostolate seriously.[8]

Schools are places for serious intellectual work; classrooms are places for teachers who because they have understood something can convey it to another by speaking to him and with him. That

[8] See Emile Mersch, "The Teacher of Religion, His Interior Life and Teaching," in *Lumen Vitae,* XIII (January, 1958), p. 27: "As we are dealing with teaching, with intellectual acquirements, it is in the sphere of knowledge that we must unite ourselves with Him. His way of thought, the inner knowledge He has of Himself, the interior conversation which is the expression of this knowledge, all this is inserted in us with the grace of Faith."

is not the whole of Christianity, but schools and classrooms were never intended to be the whole of Christianity. Giving religious education an impossible objective under the guise of making it more important and meaningful succeeds only in destroying it for its proper function. To say that the aim of catechizing is "encounter with Christ," "total commitment," "formation of the whole man," or a variety of other formulas, sounds very impressive, but it confuses the whole of Christianity with the limited functions of religious education. In practice, this seems bound to result in one of two things. On the one hand, this leads to the denial that understanding is a legitimate end in itself, an end for which teaching is peculiarly suited and for which schools exist. This leads in turn, ironically enough, to a questioning of whether schools and teachers have any part at all here since they never do achieve what is being demanded of them. The other alternative is that the schools and teachers really set about doing these things, namely, *to make* Christians, *to form* students' freedom, *to enable* students to encounter Jesus. On the surface, these schools could appear to have considerable success, but their long-term results would be the most disastrous of all.

The work of the catechist is a work of helping men to attain an understanding of the Christian life. To ask whether this is all that he does and whether he does not do something more than that, shows little appreciation of either the difficulty or the importance of helping men to know the truth. It is a truth which must be assimilated by flesh and blood and gradually brought to conscious understanding. My proposal has nothing to do with a bloodless rationalism or a theological system attainable only by the most gifted students. My demand for a thoroughly intellectual teaching is a demand to work with the intelligence of the child according to the actual, concrete structures of his understanding. Any teacher who has ever succeeded in teaching anything well knows how to make this distinction.

71

The depreciation of "mere knowledge," instruction, and intellectual assent stems from the assumption that feeding words into little children's heads is an intellectual procedure. This is a most remarkable assumption. To dissect the Trinity into a maze of theological terms for a seven- (or a seventeen-) year-old child is not mere instruction as opposed to formation, not mere knowledge as opposed to formation, not mere knowledge as opposed to faith, not intellectual assent as opposed to an appeal to the whole man. If there is one thing certain about such a procedure, it is its utter disregard for the intelligence of the child and its failure to achieve in him any intellectual understanding.

Since I am just as opposed to this kind of teaching as those who attack it as "too intellectual," it might appear that there is question here only of terminology. I do not think that this is so. Those who depreciate the centrality of knowledge in catechizing are equating knowledge with words and concepts that exist "inside" man and do not affect the "real world." I deny that such an identification should be made, and furthermore I deny that it is an accident that it has been made. We are sure of what we are against, but that is not enough. The failure to get at the roots of the problem and to find a true Christian understanding threatens to vitiate all attempts to improve religious education.

In the work of catechizing we do not have a choice between knowledge and something other than or beyond knowledge. We do indeed have a choice, but it is between a superficial knowledge which does not come to grips with the real, and a knowledge that is a standing open to the truth, which because it does face the real is always on the way, fixed in its fundamental option for truth but ever searching for a more adequate understanding. Instead of taking upon itself the salvation of students, catechetics ought to get on with its proper business, which is a very small yet highly important function of the whole Church. For the catechist, this means recognizing that his is not the divine task of

72

saving children, but rather the human task of freeing men for life in the Spirit by awakening intelligence and freedom. Every good teacher recognizes that he can do only a little to change the direction of a child's life. On this point, however, what Buber has written of the teacher could be applied with particular force to the catechist:

> Among this infinity of form-giving forces the educator is only one element among innumerable others, but distinct from them all by his *will* to take part in the stamping of character and by his *consciousness* that he represents in the eyes of the growing person a certain *selection* of what is, the selection of what is "right," of what *should* be. It is in this will and this consciousness that his vocation as an educator finds its fundamental expression. From this the genuine educator gains two things: first, humility, the feeling of being only one element amidst the fullness of life, only one single existence in the midst of all the tremendous inrush of reality on the pupil; but secondly, self-awareness, the feeling of being therein the only existence that *wants* to affect the whole person, and thus the feeling of responsibility for the selection of reality which he represents to the pupil.[9]

Human knowledge is never a private inner experience; it cannot exist without objective expression. The stress on the participating subject taking part in the revelational knowledge is not in opposition to the objective side of revelation. The objective expression of knowledge in concepts, gestures, and words is not the whole of knowledge, but is indispensable to the knowing process.[10] There is no need to choose in the teaching of religion between intellectual penetration and bodily expressions. The adventure toward human understanding must be an appeal to freedom through the objective and bodily realms in which man lives his life.

The statements that are used and must be used in awakening

[9] Martin Buber, "The Education of Character," in *Between Man and Man* (Boston, Beacon Paperback, 1955), p. 106.

[10] See Karl Rahner, "Development of Dogma," in *Theological Investigations,* I, p. 64.

this knowledge should be presented as important and as expressive of the truth. However, the impression should not be given that they are or could be exhaustive of the truth. The student himself ought to be encouraged to rethink his own Christian life in relation to his own cultural world. To denigrate these imperfect attempts at expressing conceptually and verbally what revelation means for him does not do justice to the importance of the reflexivity and objectification that is necessary for adult believers.[11] The world looks to Christian believers for concrete proposals, and these cannot be arrived at unless Christians begin to think and to think hard. Reflection upon the meaning of revelation is not the prerogative of the first believers but is the duty of all believers.

Continued reflection upon Christian revelation necessarily creates a continually changing terminology. Those in catechetical work must use a living language, one which emerges from life and thought and one which may evoke some response in another. "It is possible to cause a barrier to communication by words of another kind, words that in a former age were emotionally loaded, but now are devoid of emotional content."[12] When this has happened to language, it is not possible to restore its meaning and power by holding conferences on "the problem of language" or by compiling larger handbooks of definitions. There is no hope for the vivifying of a religious language except in a style of living more deeply Christian and in a renewed, intensive thinking on a theological level.

The language that is required for bringing to fuller reflexive consciousness the student's participation in revelation cannot only be simple language or theologically accurate language—though it should be both of these. But there must be a language that is

[11] See Liégé, *Consider Christian Maturity*, pp. 31–32.
[12] *Catholic Catechism. Book II. Teacher's Book,* issued by Australian Bishops' Committee for Education (Sydney, E. J. Dwyer, 1963), p. 64.

74

born of the times and speaks to the child of a particular age and social milieu. All of the resources of language are necessary for an effective inquiry into revelation: poetic and imaginative language, technical and scientific language, the simplest but profoundest language that is deeply embedded in the human.[13]

This age, however, is very distrustful of language. Words have been used too often in modern times to lie, to trick, to propagandize, to manipulate. Students do not want to hear that it is a great thing to worship God, they want to see and experience a Christian community that through song and prayer manifests unmistakably that Christian worship means something. They do not want to be told that charity is the form of all virtues, they want charity in the flesh. Unless students can find that the words are reflections of the lives of the teachers, then all attempts to avoid ending in verbalism will prove futile.

The child is in contact with the world by far more than his hearing. The objectification of his own understanding of revelation must be more than verbal. It must begin on a pre-verbal level in small children using the simple elements of their own lives (rather than vicarious experience) as the basis for their creative expressions. It must ultimately pass to a supra-verbal level wherein the adult recognizes the incapacity of words to express the meaning of revelation to himself or another. "The time comes when speaking is not enough, when the witness of the whole person is imperative, as in married love, in politics, in the apostolate, in martyrdom."[14]

[13] See Edmond Barbotin, "Connaissance rationelle et éducation de la foi," in *Documentation catéchestique,* XLVI (1960), pp. 29–30; Congar, *Jesus Christ,* pp. 51–53.

[14] Hans Urs von Balthasar, *Word and Revelation* (New York, Herder and Herder, 1964), p. 106.

VII.

The Bible and Religion Teaching

THE clearest point of agreement in Catholic and Protestant writing on religious education today is the central place to be occupied by holy Scripture. Protestantism has usually maintained the primary and indispensable role of the Bible, while Catholic writing has only in recent years recognized—or rediscovered—the unique role which the Bible should play in catechetical work. As a result of the advances in Catholic exegesis and also through the influence of liturgical and ecumenical movements, there has been a great rush to reinstate the Bible in its proper place in Catholic religious education. This undertaking in catechetics needs the careful direction not only of exegesis, but also of a theology that understands the place of the Bible in the total revelational process. It would be most unfortunate if the Bible were badly used in this attempt to revivify religion teaching. There is some evidence that this is in fact happening. Reflecting upon the catechetical situation throughout the United States, Gerard S. Sloyan writes: "We have discovered 'salvation history' which all too often means neither more nor less than Bible history on new and better terms. It is scholarly. It is enlightened. But it is mere Bible history which saves no one. . . . We have discovered the Bible lately, and we rush impetuously to share

76

our treasure without taking time to do with it what the church has always done: teach Christ from it."[1]

It is said in catechetical literature that the task of catechesis is the transmission of the "word of God." In the Christian era the phrase "word of God" refers first of all to the Son, the personal Word who comes from the Father. The Bible is also in some sense the "word of God," but by considering the Scriptures in relation to Christ we come to realize that the "word of God" always comes to us received and incarnated in the human. Thus the biblical word is a divine-human word, which, like Christ, cannot cease to be either divine or human without being exhausted of its significance. For catechetical purposes, therefore, we must be careful to avoid treating the biblical text on the one hand as words of God fallen from the heavens, and on the other hand as only a human record of a previous revelatory event.[2]

The Bible is not a collection of revealed truths, divine pronouncements of words revealed from on high. God did not reveal the statements of the Bible; he revealed himself. Though I do not advocate a less important place for the Bible in religious education, I must point out once more that revelation does not take place in a book but in the conscious, free experience of men in community. It does not seem accurate to recommend the use of the Bible on the principle that it is God's original revelation. The wonderful works of God and the story of the wonderful works of God are not exclusive of one another, but neither are they identical. God did not communicate truths through a biblical narrative; he acted—and still acts—in the lives of people. The Bible is an indispensable element in the process of revelation, but it must not be confused with the whole.

[1] Gerard S. Sloyan, "Catechetical Crossroads," in *Religious Education,* LIX (March, 1964), pp. 148–149.

[2] See Luis Alonso Schökel, *The Inspired Word* (New York, Herder and Herder, 1965), pp. 49–90.

Though I deny, then, that the Bible is the collection of original, revealed truths from God, I do not place the biblical words outside of the revelatory relationship of God and man. To speak on the one hand of revelation as event, and then on the other hand to call the Bible a witness to revelation, might give some people the impression that Scripture is a human though inspired record extraneous to revelation itself. This notion can arise only if we think of words as things which stand for other things instead of recognizing that human experience and thought are born and expressed in language. Man is the being who speaks. God reveals himself to human beings, and because it is man who is the revelatory partner, the revelational process could not help but have a verbal element. It is a divine-human word that testifies from within a divine-human experience that issues from a divine-human relationship.

The Catholic Church in its traditional doctrine of inspiration continues to teach that God not only intends thoughts or truths in holy Scripture, but that he is in some sense the *author* of the text. Scripture, therefore, is not a source book of Christian truths, the imagery and style of which can be set aside in favor of the "revealed truths" taught in Scripture. Strangely enough, those who try to exalt Scripture by identifying it with revelation end up by disregarding the words and imagery of Scripture, demythologizing these away in order to get at the *real* revelation. But when Scripture is given its proper but limited role in revelation, there is little problem in accepting the whole Bible for what it is: inspired literature. Its imagery, symbolism, and vocabulary are what belong to such literature. It is not the task of religion teachers to strip down Genesis, Hosea, or Job and explain what the author really wished to say. "A literary man ordinarily says what he wishes to say."[3] It was out of the experience of the com-

---

[3] *Ibid.*, p. 162; see also Karl Rahner, "Inspiration in the Bible," in *Inquiries* (New York, Herder and Herder, 1964), pp. 49–53.

munity of Israel and the apostolic Church that this literature grew up. It is in the beautiful imagery of the Bible that the contemporary Christian community can express and deepen its faith.

There was an inherent danger in these literary productions. When words expressive of God's revelation are spoken from human lips it is quite evident that their function is to mediate the intersubjective communion which is revelation. But when the words were written down in books (and precisely insofar as the words were not recognized as *literature*), it became easy for the human mind to reduce revelation to a collection of objects ouside of man. When man is confronted with a written text rather than a person, he is more tempted to take up the attitude of a disinterested spectator who can consider the significance of the statements from a neutral point of view.

It is even possible completely to overlook the fact that Scripture is an invitation on the part of a believing community to join in their belief. With no recognition of the faith and communal character of Scripture it is not realized that the ability to understand what is written depends in part on the moral attitude of the reader. When Scripture is so reduced to written statements of objective facts, "it becomes impossible for the subject to face the decision with passion, least of all with infinitely interested passion."[4] Thus we can see why Christianity has always accorded an important place to preacher and teacher because it is through them that the biblical word emerges from personal and communal experience to become for the hearer God's invitation to believe.

One of the most frequently made assertions in contemporary catechetical writing is that revelation is not a collection of truths or statements, but that it is a series of historical events. These

[4] Søren Kierkegaard, *Concluding Unscientific Postscript* (Princeton, Princeton University Press, 1941), p. 32.

concrete, historical events, it is said, are to be found in the Bible; therefore, religious education must take its starting point from the Bible. I have agreed that revelation does take place in historical events and that the Bible has an intrinsic and indispensable role to play in the process. But there resides in these statements about the Bible both an ambiguity of meaning and an unadmitted difficulty. The events in the history of Israel and events in the history of the primitive Church are events of the past. They cannot be made present events, nor are they the concrete, personal events in which God is now revealing. The biblical text that issued from Israel and the primitive Church and that is given to the child today is not a concrete, historical event. It is at the obvious level a set of statements descriptive of events which are quite removed from the child's life. To presume that the teaching is concrete, personal, and relevant simply because the Bible is the text is an unjustified assumption. "A dull historical recital can be as meaningless to youth as a revelling in formulas."[5] It surely is not difficult to make the Old Testament as abstract and irrelevant as the Baltimore Catechism. No set of statements, even if it be the inspired word of God, can guarantee that Christian revelation is being awakened and understood. The identification of revelation with any written doctrine whether catechetical or biblical can only be disastrous.

The Old Testament history and the history of the life of Jesus are meant to function as an interpretive norm for the student's own life. But in order that these biblical accounts should make an impact on the student's life, his own history has to be rich enough and conscious enough to be moved toward finding such a norm of understanding. The Bible itself may help to stir up the desire for conscious understanding of human life, but the work of the religion teacher must not be narrowly restricted to

[5] Gerard S. Sloyan, "What Should Children's Catechisms Be Like?," in *Pastoral Catechetics*, p. 44.

dealing only with matters biblical. Education in general and religious education in particular must be rich in human awareness, beauty, and symbolism for men to be able to read the Bible with full appreciation.

While I would insist, then, on the imagery, language, and style of the biblical writing as uniquely advantageous to religion teaching, I would also maintain that it may be better to approach the teaching of religion from a variety of starting points bringing in Scripture at various places. Holy Scripture, beyond the relationship which it has to the universal Church, has a variety of relationships to the individual's life of faith. Scripture can awaken faith, it can express a faith already present, it can deepen a faith for the future. It can be a jumping off point for the teaching of Christian faith, it can be a summary of what has been taught, it is always at least implicitly a guide for what is being taught.[6]

Revelation happens in the free personal existence of man in the present community. That man should recognize this it is necessary that he be confronted with the biblical text. The movement is primarily from people to text rather than vice versa. This should not be confused, however, with a "problem-centered" teaching in which the Bible is justified only by its capacity to supply answers to "felt needs." The more profound needs of man's situation are discovered as he faces the biblical testimony which may speak a different word than what man was expecting or thought he desired.[7] It remains true nevertheless that God's revelation happens in people, and therefore anything that is truly personal and humanizing can be used to bring out the sense of God's revelation. A narrow biblicist approach might

[6] See Jean-Paul Labelle, "The Use of the Bible during the Pre-Catechumenate," in *Teaching All Nations,* II (July, 1965), pp. 309–319.
[7] See Sherrill, *op. cit.,* pp. 106–107, 181–182.

81

produce many beautiful, imaginative, and powerful notions, but these would remain outside the mainstream of contemporary life in a "sacred history" isolated from the real drives and motivations of men's lives.

The statement now frequently made in Catholic theological writing that "holy Scripture contains the whole revelation" is in some sense undoubtedly true; but for catechetical purposes this statement must not be taken simplistically.[8] Catechetical writers are wont to praise the unity and simplicity of the Bible in its conveyance of the meaning of revelation to young people. The praise is well deserved, but the simplicity should not be thought of as one in which simple answers are ready-made for application to the present. Grappling with the complexities of human life has sometimes been avoided by quoting scriptural texts that reduce all problems to black and white precepts. "In reading the Gospel we may be subconsciously seduced, by the very charm of its simplicity, into an ill-judged narrowmindedness, not appreciating the true humanity of that dialogue which God does really hold with mankind."[9]

It is not the clearest use of language to say that "all revelation is contained in Scripture." The Word who is the fullness of God's revelation can be found by reading holy Scripture, but he is not "contained" there in any usual sense of the word. Furthermore, the Catholic believes that although Scripture is a uniquely inspired testimony to the revelation of God in Christ, the entire Church can be revelatory of God. "It is clear then that all catechesis, in whatever form, has as its starting point the living Word at work in the Church in the present, made manifest in the various forms of her life: sacraments, commandments, formulas of faith. It is a Word that has been partially expressed in

[8] See Moran, *Theology of Revelation,* pp. 106–110.
[9] Chenu, *op. cit.,* p. 8.

Scripture."[10] This last sentence does not contradict the thesis that "all revelation is in Scripture," but it recognizes that the Word cannot be confined to words, and that biblical words are the precipitate of a revelatory experience not fully expressible in words. It follows from this that preachers and teachers of holy Scripture must be attentive to the situation of their hearers, must recognize the truth already present among people, and must work to create a wide field of human understanding for proclaiming the one who gives more than human meaning to man.

The text of holy Scripture has its full meaning against the background of the contemporary human situation and the whole tradition of interpretation. Each text has its place in a pattern of activity on the part of God so that the whole of the Bible is the context of interpretation for the part. Catechetical writing correctly demands that students be shown the whole pattern and that each part be fitted into the whole. However, it should not be decided on the basis of some absolute standard what quantity of biblical information is necessary or useful for particular students. One can overdo the emphasis on the structure and detail of the "plan of salvation." More may be accomplished by concentrating upon a very small section of Scripture without always worrying about the big picture and the grand plan.

The personal nature of Christian revelation and the organic structure of the Bible centered on Christ imply that there is a dynamism inherent to the understanding of revelation. Consequently, one need not say everything. The contemporary catechetical problem is not that teachers do not cover everything, but that they cover too much, a problem that has not been alleviated by new approaches which often pile up more and more half digested biblical material. If we multiply images of Christ,

[10] Joseph Colomb, "The Use of the Bible in Teaching the Church's Faith," in *Modern Catechetics,* p. 17.

the Church, and the sacraments, this may do little to deepen students' appreciation and understanding of revelation. We need not get them to understand everything; what they really need is to understand *anything* about Christianity. From there they could largely take it on their own.

The understanding of holy Scripture requisite for catechists is bound up with the literal meaning intended by the author. Neither preaching nor catechizing can be content with a fanciful or allegorical interpretation for their own purposes. The findings of modern biblical scholarship should be of immense help to catechists. This new biblical knowledge includes not only the scientific exegesis of individual texts, but an understanding of the texts in relation to the "theology" which characterizes an individual book or writer. The catechist need not get too deeply involved in the continuing controversy over "senses of Scripture." He can be sure of at least one thing, that the Church especially in her liturgy has never limited the use of Scripture to the meaning that was clearly present to the author's mind. The Church, perceiving intuitively that history is fully understood only at its end, has found through the end point of her history more in the texts than the apparent literal meaning. "Her chief ancient principle is not allegory, not paraenesis, not 'spiritual sense,' but typology, the idea that a great variety of things in men's lives stand for God, and of these Jesus Christ is the chief, and many persons and things in turn stand for him."[11]

In teaching the Old Testament it is important to take seriously the real development that went on in Israelite understanding. When this progressive understanding is neglected the Old Testament becomes converted into a system of timeless truths. This will happen even though the text is covered chronologically and

[11] Gerard S. Sloyan, "Catechetical Crossroads," *loc. cit.,* p. 148; see also Joseph Gelineau, "The Nature and Role of Signs in the Economy of the Covenant," in *Worship,* XXXIX (November, 1965), pp. 546–547.

84

many historical and imaginative details are added. Let it be made clear that revelation happens in human life and then it will not be difficult for students to grasp the fact of gradual growth in understanding, the inclusion of various levels of interpretation and reinterpretation, and the use of many forms of literature.

The dimension of an historical progression should always have some part in catechizing, but there should be much room for flexibility in the ordering of material for teaching. The Old Testament, in whatever order it is taught, ought to cast some light of understanding on the student's life. A simple, linear-historical methodology would not generally be advisable. Other approaches to the Old Testament must be combined with a chronological one to make sure that there is a movement between text and student, a dialectic of integration and transformation.

At first glance, the history of the Old Testament seems far removed from the lives of present-day students. The Christian believes, however, that the history reflected there is the history of every man and that the Old Testament is itself a history of religious education. These ideas are beautifully summarized in the *Constitution on Divine Revelation:* "The books of the Old Testament . . . reveal to all men the knowledge of God and of man and the ways in which God, just and merciful, deals with men. These books, though they also contain some things which are incomplete and temporary, nevertheless show us true divine pedagogy. These same books, then, give expression to a lively sense of God, contain a store of sublime teachings about God, sound wisdom about human life, and a wonderful treasury of prayer."[12] The Old Testament, therefore, is not only the history of Israel, but the history of God's dealing with man. Every man can find something of his own life's history reflected in the drama of the Israelite history, although teachers should beware of attempting an easy concordance. What is needed for the Old

[12] Chapter IV, Article 15.

Testament to come alive is not a superficial step-by-step "application" of it to the student, but real appreciation for it as magnificent literature and deep reflection upon it in relation to the contemporary complex society.

One thing that can help in understanding the Old Testament and its significance is a concern for the personalities of ancient Israel. The teacher should expend more time and effort in trying to convey some sense of the personal lives of the great leaders, the prophets, or the poor of Israel, rather than concentrating upon impersonal facts, dates, and prescriptions. This is advocated not only on psychological grounds, but on the basis of a theology of revelation; for it is in the person living in community that God reveals himself and not in some scheme of historical facts.[13]

The most important single principle for organizing Old Testament teaching is its relation to the person of Christ. Although some progression from the state of slavery to that of sonship perdures in the Christian life, a fundamental and irreversible newness has been introduced with Christ. As Vatican II has pointed out, the Christian always reads the Old Testament through the prism of its fulfillment and conclusion in Christ. "God, the inspirer and author of both Testaments, wisely arranged that the New Testament be hidden in the Old and the Old be made manifest in the New. For though Christ established the new covenant in His blood, still the books of the Old Testament with all of their parts, caught up into the proclamation of the Gospel, acquire and show forth their full meaning in the New Testament and in turn shed light on it and explain it."[14]

The place of Christ is so central that it would be unwise to structure Old Testament teaching before this prior relation is

---

[13] See Marc Oraison, *Love or Constraint* (Glen Rock, Paulist Press, 1961), p. 150; Vincent Novak, "Teaching the Old Testament," *The Bible Today,* I (April, 1963), p. 376.

[14] *Constitution on Divine Revelation,* Chapter IV, Article 16.

86

established. This means not a perfunctory glance at Christ in the first chapter of books on the Old Testament, but a continuing interplay between present society, the figure of Christ, and the Old Testament. The Old Testament retains its present actuality not by its events transcending time, but by its having been taken up into the history of the Lord Jesus who remains present in his Church as God's revelation. Whatever is taught, the Old Testament should be an ever present background and the New Testament within the Church the foreground.[15] On the basis of this principle I would strongly question the value of new programs in high schools and colleges that devote the first year almost exclusively to the Old Testament and follow this with a year of New Testament exegesis. I see no justification for these programs either psychologically or theologically. Many places are already reaching the point of diminishing returns on the newness aspect. Surely there are more imaginative approaches than ploughing through the books of the Bible one after the other.

We have returned to the central principle that all teaching on Christian revelation is at least implicitly a pointing toward Jesus Christ who is the revelatory communion of God and man. The teacher can point to Jesus by many diverse ways, but of these the New Testament is unique in kind and indefectible in validity. The personality of the Lord must become familiar to teachers and students through prayerful study of the New Testament writings. Teachers, it is to be hoped, are attaining through modern biblical research a clearer picture of the majestic figure of the historical Jesus dying and rising as the hope of mankind.

In trying to give some understanding of the New Testament record of revelation it should be even more obvious than with the Old Testament that the unity of presentation and the base of historical certainty is not a series of events, but a person and a

[15] See Franz Schreibmayr, "The Faith of the Church and Formal Doctrinal Instruction," in *Modern Catechetics*, p. 61.

community. The intention of the New Testament writers was clearly not to present all the "revealed truths" that Christians need to know. They put together a variety of remembrances which are unified in pointing to the person Christ. The authors and editors of the New Testament apparently exercised a good deal of liberty, "selecting some things from the many which had been handed on by word of mouth or in writing, reducing some of them to a synthesis, explaining some things in view of the situation of their churches . . ."[16]

In the New Testament, the apostles do not claim to say everything: they wish to say enough that men may continue to believe and believing may have life in his name (Jn. 20:31). In contrast to the Old Testament prophets, they do not claim to speak the word of God, but only to be the servants of the Word (Jn. 21:25). Instead of giving us a perfected system they allow us to follow their psychological processes as they reflected upon the life of Jesus from the vantage point of Easter-Pentecost. If religion teachers follow the sequence of New Testament development there will be fewer problems on the historicity of individual events in a "life of Christ." This, however, is less a methodological or curriculum principle and more a principle of understanding which, because the teacher possesses it, will influence his teaching. That modern biblical criticism has this direct relation to catechetics is not so surprising given the fact that the New Testament developed in large part from theological reflection upon the life of Jesus for catechetical and liturgical reasons.

The fact that the Church used several forms of literature to transmit her belief in this historical person does not present great difficulty to younger minds. At least it will not unless they are first schooled in a fundamentalism which makes the New Testament a collection of factual accounts recorded by disinterested

---

[16] *Constitution on Divine Revelation*, Chapter V, Article 19; see also Alonso Schökel, *op. cit.*, p. 109.

spectators. But taken as brilliant insights into the personality of the man who received God's self-donation in revelatory communion, the New Testament takes on an exciting and fascinating character which makes it speak to contemporary man as no perfected system of reason could. "It is enough to penetrate into the soul of the twentieth-century man in order to cause that deep water to spring forth from which will be reborn, recreated by grace, the man of the Bible, the new and eternal man, in Jesus."[17]

[17] Moeller, loc. cit., p. 156.

VIII.

The Student and Continuing Revelation

I have insisted that the phrase "the student is now living in salvation history" is not to be taken as a figure of speech or as expressive of the fact that Christian revelation is to be "applied" to the present. If faith is to be personal, if Christianity is to be transformatory of man, if the Lord Jesus is not to be thought of as having abandoned his Church, then the continued happening of revelation in the Christian era must be understood in all strictness. Catechetical and liturgical terminology, I have pointed out, has in many respects outdistanced theological writing which has little struggled with this delicate and complex issue. Catholic theology has generally been slow to appreciate the question and therefore has not seriously faced the needed reconciliation. There is on the one hand the teaching of the Church on the "closing of revelation" in apostolic times, and on the other hand the necessary affirmation that revelation as a personal event, an action of God with his people, must be a present reality and a continuing occurrence. This irresolvable tension of fulfillment and continuing process runs throughout Catholic theology, but it is surprising how little it has been examined in considering the nature of revelation itself. Catechetical and liturgical writing seem to have reached a formulation of the matter without having worked out the theology to support it. They stand in need of

90

a theological foundation for their assertions if the words are not to become empty shells.

Catechesis is concerned with the understanding of God's revelation now taking place in the student's life. The whole of the exposition could be summed up in the reality of the *Church* if we understand the word "Church" broadly enough.[1] Modern theology has done much to broaden and deepen our understanding of the Church. In particular, there has been a unification of the theology of Christ, the Church, and the chief liturgical activities through the single notion of sacrament. This undoubtedly has been a gain for theology and has provided a richer context for teachers to work within. But the rapid introduction of these ideas and terms into catechetical writing is another matter. It is becoming commonplace to find in books used on elementary and secondary levels such formulations as "The Church is the sacrament of Christ as Christ is the sacrament of God." This terminology, unless preceded and accompanied by basic reorientation of thinking, is liable to be taken for a playing around with words. We mistakenly think that we are succeeding with new terminology because students can get some meaning from the words. What we fail to see is that this meaning no more connects with their real lives than did that of the old terms. Worse still, the new terminology might inhibit real theological thinking later because students have been through all those words already. The catechist who is inadequately prepared theologically tends to teach the most theology and to use the most theologically laden language. The teacher, on the other hand, who really understands ecclesiology will realize that his task with younger students is not to give them the latest ideas and terms of ecclesi-

[1] See *Directoire de pastorale catéchetique à l'usage des diocèses de France*, p. 17: "Catechesis is *always a manifestation of the mystery of the Church.* . . . Catechesis is always tied to liturgical celebration and the witness of charity of the Church."

ologists, but to introduce the child or adolescent through an unlimited variety of images and experiences to the meaning of the Church.

For the students to appreciate their Church, to accept a teaching authority within that Church, and to desire to participate in the Church's official worship, all depends upon their eventual realization that Jesus Christ is a living person, that God spoke to him, and that in the glorifying act of raising him God continues to speak the Word of his love. If that never emerges in the students' understanding, all other "explanations" of the Church's life and doctrine will never be intelligible. If they do not believe in a living Lord it is futile to try to explain the Mass to them as an act of the past somehow happening again, to explain moral decisions as applications of abstract laws to present situations, to explain dogmas as the deduction of "revealed truths" from a deposit of faith. All of these explanations falter or they fail to relate to the real lives of people unless revelation is conceived to be a present reality, present because Jesus Christ is living and present. All explanations in Christianity must have their root in Christ, who is in the strictest sense of the words, the Sacrament, the Law, and the Revelation.[2]

The Church as a whole is the revelational act of God, the visible and social manifestation of his presence among men. However, the external structure and outward form of the Church is only signatory of revelation. Like all symbolic expressions, the bodying forth of revelation into the world both veils and unveils the reality symbolized. For men who can penetrate appearances and distinguish between good and bad, it should be possible to

[2] See Jean Mouroux, *The Mystery of Time* (New York, Desclée, 1964), p. 177: "In the Christian faith, eschatological time is rooted completely in the presence of the Risen Christ. It is not rooted in a divine promise or a divine decision, but in a *Person Who is Present.* Christ is "seated at the Father's right hand," not to await the end from afar, but to pour forth the Holy Spirit (Acts 2:33), and thus fulfill the role of eternal mediator."

appreciate the Church as the sacramental revelation of God. The Church, despite the sinful wounds she bears, is truly a miracle of God's love, a standard raised up among the nations.

Young people, however, and especially adolescents, find it difficult to differentiate between the essential goodness of an institution, project, or person, and the always present weakness and failure of men. To accept the Church, that is, to live in the society united to God in Christ, students must be helped to see the Church as truly revealing God amidst all the human weakness. "It all depends, therefore, on making visible to the children the beauty, the compactness, the indestructibility of the Catholic Church, its authority in proclaiming doctrines, its wealth of heroic virtue and holiness."[3] This perception of the Church as God's revelation cannot be brought about, least of all in our day, by hiding the faults and sins of Christianity and by answering every objection to the Church with whitewashing apologetic. The teacher must have enough faith to suppose that if the Church is seen in truth with all of her greatness and weakness, it will be a sufficiently attractive vision to bring students to accept the Church. There is no other approach left open to us today. "The truth cannot impose itself except by virtue of its own truth, as it makes its entrance into the mind at once quietly and with power."[4]

Young people must eventually come to distinguish between the divine call which sounds through the Church and the sins of men which scar the Church. This fact, however, does not excuse us from trying to make everything in the Church "speak." Scripture and liturgy can be heard very effectively only if there is much else in the Church, in the school, in the religion class, and in the attitude of teachers that speaks of God. More precisely stated, this means that all who teach the young must be con-

[3] Jungmann, *Handing on the Faith*, p. 249.
[4] *Declaration on Religious Liberty*, Article I.

cerned with letting God speak through them and must be attentive to the many factors operative here. Sometimes a word or gesture speaks more than long explanations; sometimes, too, small obstacles can stand in the way of religious understanding. "In a really living Church there is perhaps nothing inconsequential at all."[5]

Striving for renewal in the Church in order to bring out the full revelatory character of the Church is the responsibility of all Christians. There must be educated a laity that is intelligent, critical, and articulate. They must love the Church enough to work for her renewal and be ready to enter into fruitful dialogue with authority in the Church. The work of renewal and reform is not something demanded only by the failings of this age. The demand for continuous renewal and adaptation is solidly based upon the nature of revelation itself and its continuing reality in a divine-human Church. "The Church's special importance as a sign and revelation demands that she return again and again to the sources of biblical authenticity and show herself in forms that clearly and simply manifest her authenticity."[6]

The Church is not only an institution with a determined and stable structure. It is at the same time a community with a history constituted by events and actions. With varying degrees of intensity and completeness the Church realizes and expresses her nature in the historical order. The individual within the Church must face the question of his own belief at particular spatiotemporal points. By focusing her attention on selected moments of history, the Church brings to full awareness and expression her receptive contact with the revelatory-redemptive activity of God in Christ. The activities and words which are the most com-

[5] Karl Barth, *The Humanity of God* (London, Collins, 1961), p. 65.

[6] Edward Schillebeeckx, "The Church and Mankind," in *Concilium,* "Dogma," Volume I, *The Church and Mankind,* edited by same (Glen Rock, Paulist Press, 1965), p. 89.

plete expression of her nature were determined in a general way by Christ her founder. "For the duration of cosmic history, Christ produced certain words which are continually in the course of returning to the Father—namely, the words of preaching and the sacraments. In them, the words of grace spoken in time, in which the eternal converse of love is made audible in part to us, are spread further through time and space."[7]

The summit of God's revelatory activity in Christian time is found in the liturgy. The liturgy does not complement or parallel revelation; it is revelation: God communicating with man in Christ. Liturgy's direct orientation is worship-sanctification, but precisely in having this direction and to the degree it fulfills this purpose, it is always instructional. For centuries the religious education of the faithful took place mainly through liturgical participation. The present liturgical movement, while recognizing the vast changes in educational needs since the early Church, is attempting to make the liturgy a potent force of education once more.[8]

The liturgical act, as the high point of continuing revelation, is the paradigm or exemplar for all lesser revelatory activities in the Church. Religion teaching that takes place outside of the liturgy must reflect the spirit, structure, and content of the liturgy. It is not a matter of "putting a little liturgy into the religion course," but of steeping religion teaching in the outlook of the liturgy. When this is the context within which the religion teacher works, then the teaching will draw its strength from and be a preparation for liturgical prayer. This will be true even when there is no conscious or explicit advertence to the

[7] Michael Schmaus, *Essence of Christianity* (Chicago, Scepter, 1961), p. 200.

[8] See Josef Jungmann, *Pastoral Liturgy* (New York, Herder and Herder, 1962), pp. 325–416; see also *Constitution on the Sacred Liturgy*, Chapter I, Articles 1, 2, 5, 6, 7, 10.

95

liturgy in the teaching. The teaching of religion can itself become a kind of prayer in act, a beginning of liturgical prayer.[9]

We have already looked at the role of holy Scripture in the revelational process. It may be mentioned here, however, that the liturgical use of Scripture brings out most strikingly the nature of revelation as prayerful union with God and present event within the community.[10] Herein the liturgy throws light upon what a religion class ought to be; for what the preacher of Scripture is to do, namely, search with his hearers in prayerful obedience for an understanding of what God is now asking of them, ought to characterize all religion teaching. Such an attitude is not at all incompatible with a religion teaching that is a serious intellectual endeavor. Admittedly, there is a difference of emphasis. Nevertheless, catechizing, even when carried out in a highly formalized classroom arrangement, can still originate from prayer and awaken a deep, worshipful attitude without always rushing directly at it.

The liturgical use of Scripture shows that the revelatory word is a present, personal, communal word that mediates the union of God and man. The catechist, just as the preacher, by the present spoken word within the community, brings to expression the faith that is already there and thereby deepens that faith for the future. For God to speak through catechetical instruction it is imperative that there be teachers who have personally and prayerfully assimilated the meaning of Scripture and who can create the atmosphere in which the teaching of Scripture can be received as revelatory of God.

In the Catholic understanding of public worship, the spoken, scriptural word leads of itself into sacramental expressions that encompass the verbal element in bodily and social activities. In

9 See *Directoire de pastoral catéchetique à l'usage des diocèses de France*, p. 40, n. 82.
10 See Grasso, *Proclaiming God's Message*, pp. 47–68.

catechizing there is also a taking hold of man that should find visible and sacramental expression. This need not always be the sacraments in the narrow sense of the word. Catholicism has always made provision for "lesser sacraments." All personal and symbolic gestures expressive of God's graciousness and man's receptivity are steps toward the full living of revelation and the participation in liturgical prayer. For a Christian, all these prayerful gestures find their culmination in the external and social acts which specify the Church, that is, the sacraments. The liturgy, therefore, and most particularly the sacraments, necessarily becomes central to a reflection upon Christian revelation. Such a demand is based not upon the desire for a good pedagogical gimmick or the wish to give a pious twist to religion teaching, but upon a theological understanding of the nature of revelation.[11]

The ultimate meaning of liturgy for religious education is not to be sought in explanations of the liturgy, but in the praying of the liturgy. There is some danger in all the talk today which makes liturgy "one of the four ways" to approach the teaching of religion.[12] The liturgy must never become a mere means or tool for the use of teachers. The liturgy cannot be a teacher unless it first be itself: communal worship. But this in turn implies respect for the freedom of the individual. If schools and teachers live by manipulation, then anything can become a manipulative instrument, including the liturgy. In some places where a manipulative mentality remains strong, the liturgy is superficially adapted to the supposed needs and desires of the students and it is then wielded as a persuasive technique. Teachers soon come to conclude: "This liturgical movement is useless. We tried the

[11] See Hélène Lubienska de Lenval, *The Whole Man at Worship* (New York, Desclée, 1961), p. 80: "The strange thing is that after 2,000 years it has not penetrated more deeply into our schools, which are strongly marked by a Platonic dualism."

[12] On the so-called "four approaches" to catechizing, see below, Chapter X.

liturgy. Liturgy does not work." They are right, of course; liturgy does not work, and as soon as one tries to make it work it has already been denatured. In addition, young people are extremely suspicious these days of teachers wielding divine instruments. They sense very quickly that someone is trying to con them. They are being given the hard sell, which is the final reason that they should not buy.

A great respect for the freedom of the students must be maintained along with the attempt to introduce them to a meaningful and attractive liturgy. Facile adaptations to contemporary needs and to the mentality of the young could give them the impression that they have experienced all that the liturgy has to offer when in fact only the beginning work is being done for bringing out the revelatory power of the liturgy. All that we can do for the present is to study, to experiment, and gradually to make more meaningful the liturgical activity freely participated in. Subtle persuasions and smart advertising techniques may increase numbers for a while, but they are destructive of the ultimate end. What we hope to have eventually is freely committed Christian people who express their freedom by joining with the worshiping community. But painful as the fact may be, there is no way that one can directly make this come about.[13]

To whatever extent young Christians exercise their freedom to participate in liturgical prayer, they will be educated in a way that the formal, didactic learning can never duplicate. It is at prayer that the Church learns in every age how to serve and be served by humanity. It is in the liturgy that the individual participant finds a unique school of Christian faith. The revelation of God in Christ ought to be found everywhere in the Christian life, but it is in the Eucharist that God is most perfectly revealed to

[13] See Gabriel Moran, "The Freedom of the Sons of God," in *Twenty-Fifth North American Liturgical Week. The Challenge of the Council: Person, Parish, World*, XXV (1964), pp. 171–172.

them. "The student has to meet Christ, really meet him. There are many places to do that: in one's neighbor, in one's enemy, in a thousand ways in daily life. But of all these opportunities only the encounter in the Eucharist is the *summit* compared to which all other meetings are lower stages on the slope."[14]

Thus the liturgy supplies the culmination of religious instruction as well as the spirit and structure which should carry throughout all religion teaching. In addition to these two relationships, there is a third and lesser relation between liturgy and religious instruction. The elements used in liturgical worship form a language which can be used in extra-liturgical teaching. This is a language adapted to the capacities of all people, but especially the simple and unlettered. It is remarkable that so much effort has often been wasted in trying to teach about religious symbolism while children were not simply asked to open their eyes and look or to draw upon their own experience. Of course, one cannot deny that there has been a tragic separation of liturgical symbolism from modern life. As a result, it is only with the present renewal of liturgical rites that the catechist will begin to have the truly powerful teaching aids which the liturgy is capable of providing. But even during this rather trying period of the Church's efforts to restore the power of liturgical symbolism, the teacher can find great help in the liturgy. He would be very unwise to substitute a whole scheme of his own symbols for the Church's practice even though the latter may be in need of some change. "He who tries to discourse on baptism without paying the slightest attention to the baptismal rite and the paschal night, nor to the biblical symbols of the baptismal grace, not only makes a didactic error, but, which is worse, he parts realities which have been united by God and the Church."[15]

[14] Sloyan, "Catechetical Crossroads," *loc. cit.,* p. 149.
[15] H. M. M. Fortmann, "Towards a Development of Faith by Means of Liturgical Life," in *Faith and Commitment,* edited by Mark J. Link (Chicago, Loyola University Press, 1964), p. 62.

The proper understanding by the student of the union of word and action in liturgy is helpful in achieving the unity that is still more important, namely, that of liturgy and the whole Christian life of charity. A catechesis centered on liturgy that does not open out on all the realities of the student's life has not even succeeded in understanding the liturgy. Conversely, unless the Christian life in the world is understood to lead organically to liturgical expression, the nature of Christian morality is not grasped either.[16]

The Mass is meant to express liturgically what the rest of the student's life is in fact. The whole of Christian existence is meant to be the revelation of God's love. What is required is not to keep young people in Church as much as possible; "what is necessary is to discover and make use of those potentialities in human life which bear a special affinity to what happens in the Mass."[17] If the Mass is to be deeply revelatory of God, the charity of the Christian community must sustain a continuing revelation of God's love. Christ is always among his people who live in the love of the Spirit. It is by the students' attentiveness to their immediate surroundings that God through Christ and his Spirit speaks to them. Catechists would do better to emphasize this continuous presence which finds its full expression in the Eucharist, rather than to say that Christ is present for a few moments in the eucharistic reception and then is no longer among us "except spiritually."[18]

A teaching centered upon the personal revelation of God in

[16] See Mary Perkins Ryan, "The Focus of Catechetics," in *Worship,* XXXVII (March, 1963), pp. 233–240; Donald P. Gray, "Liturgy and Morality," in *Worship,* XXXIX (January, 1965), pp. 28–35.

[17] Karl Rahner, "The Sacrifice of the Mass and an Ascesis for Youth," in *The Christian Commitment* (New York, Sheed and Ward, 1963), p. 147.

[18] See Gerhard Boss, "Wort und Brot," in *Katechetische Blätter,* LXXXVIII (1963), p. 32; Paul De Haes, "The Presence of the Lord Christ," in *Lumen Vitae,* XX (September, 1965), pp. 435–450.

the risen Christ would give moral teaching an orientation that would dissolve most of the questions on which time is wasted in teaching morality. Rather than as a series of abstract laws that are placed mechanically upon "cases," Christian morality needs to be presented as man's creative response to historical situations through his understanding of the life, death, and resurrection of Jesus and his continued working in the Church. When revelation is assumed to be a collection of truths or principles rather than a personal communion, morality cannot help but become a static science of deductions. The resulting system of morality may appeal to young people during a certain period of their growth, but it simply cannot be the basis of an adult religious life. What we are asking for here is the furthest thing removed from an arbitrary, subjective "situation ethic." Indeed, it can be said that only a morality based upon an historical, personal, social revelation can preserve us from a "situation ethic." Nothing is more certain to lead to arbitrariness and lawlessness than the maintenance of an abstract and impersonal system of moral precepts. Not coming to grips with the real world, it must inevitably result in leaving men to make decisions on a subjective basis.[19]

In catechetical literature today there is a ceaseless demand for a better teaching of morality. Nearly everyone wants a positive morality instead of a negative one, a morality centered upon Christ and Christian charity, a morality relevant to the needs of time and place. But there is still a refusal to recognize how deep this problem goes. There is still a hope that the problem can be resolved without taking any of the necessary means. Positive morality does not come from rephrasing the commandments; charity-centered morality does not emerge from always talking about love. The first prerequisite to the emergence of an adequate

[19] See Karl Rahner, "The Question of a Formal Existential Ethics," in *Theological Investigations* (Baltimore, Helicon, 1963), II, pp. 217–234; Louis Monden, *Sin, Liberty and Law* (New York, Sheed and Ward, 1965), pp. 73–110.

101

Christian morality is a scriptural-theological understanding of the nature of revelation. Until we are ready to admit that our difficulty is at this fundamental level, we will continue to teach a negative, legalistic morality, all our resolutions to the contrary notwithstanding.

Every morally good act, every act formed by charity, is revelatory of God through Christ and the Spirit. It "contains the whole revelation." The experience of a true Christian community, the action of a single comrade or teacher can have an almost unlimited effect upon a student's life. Everything in the school and in the Church which helps the student to open his life to the awareness, service, and love of others contributes to the revelation of God in his life. "Whenever we encounter the Church's activity, its attempt to make human life more what it should be, whenever we enter the presentation of Christ's truth to men and encounter the works of charity in the Church, we encounter Christ's activity in human history."[20]

[20] Bernard Cooke, "Catechesis of the Church," in *Religious Education,* LIX (March, 1964), p. 154.

IX.

The Doctrinal Understanding
of Students

WHENEVER God reveals himself to man there is a human participant who actively receives the gift of God's loving presence. This happens even in the case of the child, though the human response here is minimal in terms of conscious awareness and adherence. The growth from childhood to maturity, however, implies the development of conceptual understanding and deliberate choice. There is no way for man to escape from this process even should he regret that he cannot continue to live in immediate and simple awareness of the real. Religious-minded men have at times attacked the rational and conceptual processes as seductions away from the real and have belittled rational formulas as unimportant in themselves.

The Church throughout her history has consistently maintained the legitimate and indispensable place of concepts and verbal formulas as the "sacraments" of revelational knowledge.[1] Precisely because Christianity is an historical religion, that is, concerned with the total human person, there is unavoidably a doctrinal element to Christian revelation. The Church, therefore,

[1] See Karl Rahner, *On Heresy* (New York, Herder and Herder, 1964), pp. 22–23.

has wisely been concerned that men should lay hold of the truth in the fullness of human understanding and has never treated lightly the doctrinal expressions of revelatory experience. This concern for the possession of correct statements has quite naturally been reflected in her catechetical instruction. The prominent place of the doctrinal is not a modern corruption but is instead a feature of catechetical instruction from the beginning. "When the Fathers of the Church are giving religious instruction, they are consistently concerned with doctrine. . . . there is a message, an idea, a conceptual content that has to be communicated."[2]

Contemporary writers often point out that the teaching of doctrinal formulas to children is no guarantee that a Christian is thereby being formed. Undoubtedly, this is true, but this should not be taken as a reason for eliminating or reducing doctrinal teaching. The basic question to be asked is whether the teacher speaks from within mystery and the student's formulas are a grasping hold of mystery, or whether the sense and meaning of mystery is not involved at all. In the former case, doctrinal formulas cannot but be a help to living the revelational life. In the latter case, the formulas are as likely to harm as to help. However, the elimination of the formulas will not be to much avail, since what is lacking is the one thing necessary, that is, the sense of "the Christian mystery."

Mystery, according to a current philosophical usage, is a whole outside of which man cannot step. It is what so involves man's life that he cannot view it as a neutral observer. He cannot comprehend it because he is comprehended by it. Rather than speak of penetrating into mystery, it would be more accurate to speak of penetrating outward from the center of mystery where man finds himself. Here every question calls into question the ques-

[2] Burghardt, "Catechetics in the Early Church: Program and Psychology," loc. cit., p. 101.

tioner himself. A man who reflects deeply upon any important personal issue finds that he cannot view the matter as an outside spectator. Neither can he find a final "solution" which would simply end the problem by untying all the knots. In questions of friendship and love, fidelity and trust, suffering and death, he finds himself encompassed by and involved in a reality that can always be further penetrated but never completely exhausted.[3]

St. Paul's use of the word "mystery" is not entirely opposed to these philosophical notions. But what is distinctive of the Pauline use of mystery is that it refers not to "being" or to a set of values but to a person: the Lord Jesus. The totality of God's actions and intentions in man's behalf constitute the pattern of an incomprehensible whole outside of which man cannot go. The key to understanding this whole set of activities is the person who realized God's intentions in the most perfect way. Every truth that man tries to enunciate about the final meaning of his life takes him into a relationship with Jesus Christ, who is related to him not as an external fact, but as the first of his brethren. The man who reflects upon the person of Jesus Christ and the person of every man in the light of Christ will find unlimited room for the formulation of true doctrinal statements. These statements, it must be recognized, even though they be true, are gropings after an inexhaustible truth which transcends man's attempts at adequate comprehension.[4]

A sense of this "Christian mystery" is the presupposition of any worth-while doctrinal teaching to children and adolescents. When catechetical writers speak of the need for students to see the whole plan or mystery of salvation, it is this context that should

[3] See Gabriel Marcel, *The Philosophy of Existentialism* (New York, Citadel Press, 1962), pp. 9–23; Bernard Murchland, "An Awareness of Mystery," in *Apostolic Perspectives,* III (October, 1958), pp. 21–23.

[4] See Barnabas Ahern *New Horizons. Studies in Biblical Theology* (Notre Dame, Fides Dome Book, 1965), pp. 75–131; Lucien Cerfaux, *Christ in the Theology of St. Paul* (New York, Herder and Herder, 1959), pp. 402–438.

be understood. Unfortunately, this "mystery of salvation" is more often being equated with involved charts and diagrams describing a series of divine interventions in the past. The history of Israel, of course, should not be excluded. But neither should one miss the deep significance of what St. Paul meant in describing the crucified and risen Lord as God's own mystery.[5] Although the word "mystery" is one of the most commonly used words in catechetical literature today, it is highly doubtful whether growth in meaningfulness has kept pace with frequency of usage. One might suspect that for many teachers mysteries are still "truths revealed by God that cannot be understood by human reason." Redefining the word "mystery" does not help much even if a biblical formulation is used. What is first needed by teachers and students is the recognition that their own lives are "mysterious," enveloped by the presence of a loving God in the transformed world of nature and other people. What must be striven for by various ways is to awaken a sense of wonder and a sympathy for persons, a readiness to accept freedom and history, and a desire to delve into the inexhaustible richness of the encompassing reality of man's relationship to God in Jesus Christ.

Basic to any sense of "Christian mystery," therefore, is the concrete, personal, intersubjective structure that must characterize it. "Christianity proclaims mysteries, absolute mysteries, which are made known only by God's revelation and still remain mysteries to the human intellect even after they have been proclaimed. But this statement does not mean that the mysteries can be transmitted to men only from the outside. They too, indeed precisely they, are spoken by God from within."[6] This understanding of mystery in Christian revelation throws some light

[5] See Grasso, "Core of Missionary Preaching," in *Teaching All Nations,* p. 42–43.
[6] Karl Rahner, "The Significance in Redemptive History of the Individual Member of the Church," in *The Christian Commitment,* p. 104.

upon procedures in catechetical work. When it is said that religion teaching should begin from something "concrete," this should not be interpreted to mean using something sensible or imaginable. The concrete reality is not a thing at all, but the personal experience of the child, especially his relation to other people. The meeting between persons is the concrete experience on which religious instruction is based.

Any development of human understanding involves conceptualization and, in some sense of the word, abstraction. The intellectual processes proper to the human condition are not at variance with the nature of Christian revelation. Violence is done to the Christian mystery only when it is supposed that the mystery can be exhausted by abstractions and replaced in practice by neutral objective statements. The abstraction, on the other hand, which is not only compatible with but demanded by Christian understanding, is one that occurs through and in concrete experience. General truths and propositions that are a necessary part of the process must be placed in subordination to the end of contemplating the real and concrete, the unique and personal.[7]

It would not be correct, therefore, to state that the procedure in catechizing is a movement from the concrete to the abstract, from particular fact to general truth. It would be more accurate to say that the procedure is from concrete to concrete, with general truths and abstractions forming part of the way. Those who are advocating an inductive teaching of religion seem to do so on the assumption that deduction as a way of teaching religion is inadequate and induction is the only alternative. The underlying assumption here is what needs challenging. Faith as a personal act and revelation as the intercommunion of persons demand a different kind of thinking than either induction or

[7] See Vincent Ayel, "Faut-il aller du concret à l'abstrait?," in *Catéchistes,* XIII (January, 1953), p. 19.

deduction. A more profound reflection upon the nature of knowledge and the structure of personal freedom is needed today if catechetical theory is to have a solid foundation for what it is trying to do.[8]

If the student has really begun to grasp the mystery "from the inside out," there are no inherent limits to the possible development of his doctrinal understanding. Far from constituting a danger, the continued reflection that springs from a life of faith cannot help but strengthen that life. On the other hand, a Christianity frozen in outdated forms and language clearly indicates that revelation is no longer a force in people's lives and that it has not really been assimilated. Every Christian to the limit of his abilities ought to be encouraged to wrestle with the difficult problems and questions posed by his allegiance to Christianity. A fidelity to personal conscience and to Christian revelation demands that no *a priori* and arbitrary limit be imposed upon doctrinal inquiry. "Much of the policy of protecting the faith of people by the exclusion of disturbing ideas is in fact a policy of jettisoning the faith of the next generation in an ill-directed attempt to salvage the faith of this."[9]

No opposition should be set up in the student's thinking between the gospel message and doctrinal understanding. Though holy Scripture should be presented as a unique book, it should also be pointed out that Scripture is a doctrinal formulation. It is the testimony of God's chosen witnesses who invite us to a reflection upon and an acceptance of the reality communicated through the Scripture. Catechetical writing that speaks of "peel-

[8] Some recent attempts to carry out such analysis may be seen in Bernard Lonergan, *Insight* (New York, Longmans, Green, 1957); Carlos Cirne-Lima, *Personal Faith* (New York, Herder and Herder, 1965); Michael Novak, *Belief and Unbelief* (New York, Macmillan, 1965); in the catechetical area proper, the work of Marcel van Caster, *The Structure of Catechetics*, is most noteworthy.

[9] Davis, "Theology and Its Present Task," *loc. cit.,* p. 112.

108

ing off the abstract terminology to get at the message of the gospel" misconstrues the task before us. It is theologically false to drive a wedge between the gospel and later doctrinal reflection as if the latter were mostly corruptive. What is needed is not less doctrinal reflection upon the gospel by students, but much more of it. Provided that the students are reflecting upon the reality testified to by holy Scripture, then the more doctrinal the teaching is, the better. To arrive at an adult faith the student must use his reflective powers so as to pass "from a faith that he had accepted quite naïvely to a faith which is now received with all of the weight of his reflective intellect and personal decision."[10]

A continuing personal reflection upon revelation will undoubtedly lead to problems which are not immediately resolvable. Teachers should beware of trying to settle all difficulties and to answer all questions whether doctrinal or moral. Few things could be more detrimental to the appreciation of Christian revelation than facile answers and superficial solutions for every question raised. Religious answers that are easily found and easily formulated are almost by definition impersonal, irrelevant, and worthless. Teachers in the past have apparently felt that the student's faith would be threatened if he did not have ready answers to every challenging question. Whether or not this may have been true in the past, the opposite would seem more likely today. Most students growing up in today's world do not want easy and final answers; they do not trust them. Proofs for this and that, refutations for every objection, explanations for failure

[10] Babin, *Crisis of Faith,* p. 117; see also Edward Schillebeeckx, "Exegesis, Dogmatics and the Development of Dogma," in *Dogmatic vs. Biblical Theology,* edited by Herbert Vorgrimler (Baltimore, Helicon, 1964), p. 132: "Speculative reason does not mean the ability to add another ingredient to the data, but the power to grasp the data in their meaningful reality, seeing their intrinsic relationship within the faith and their mutual connexions, as for instance St. Paul has himself already tried to do."

109

and error—all of these are highly suspect today. In the end they are unconvincing.

The students are correct in sensing that these are not the answers which will set them free. At best, such answers are pointers in the right direction. The more that students come to appreciate their Christian faith, the more they come to recognize that very many questions are simply not answerable from pulpit and lectern. Necessary and positive direction for leading a Christian life can be provided in churches and schools, but the precise lines of action must be found by the individual Christians in their own lives. The work of preaching and catechizing remains immensely important, but the attempt to give answers where answers cannot be found is self-defeating and self-destructive.

What we have said of holy Scripture, namely, that it yields its deepest meaning only to those who read with a prayerful attitude, holds true in regard to all the doctrinal teaching of the Church. This is why the ancient creeds as prayerful summaries of the Church's belief have always held a privileged position in catechetical instruction. "They are seen to be documents of a living faith, filled with the power of primitive teaching, permeated with the spirit of prayer, and sanctified by the blood of martyrs."[11]

It is unfortunate that at times in the history of the Church this function of the creedal formulas has been misunderstood.[12] With the loss of the personal, communal, and historical character of Christian revelation, the creed quite naturally becomes not the

[11] Schreibmayr, *loc. cit.*, p. 51.

[12] The proper function of the creeds was brought out by J. N. D. Kelly, *Early Christian Creeds* (London, 1950), pp. 1–61; see also Sloyan, "What Should Children's Catechisms Be Like?," *loc. cit.*, p. 34: "The creeds are formulated *kerygmata* or joyful announcements of all that God has done to save his people, both from their sins and for eternal life. The creedal phrases are largely biblical in original: indeed, they took their rise from the same declarations of faith that provided the framework for the gospels as we know them."

profession of faith in what God does in history, but the "revealed truths" one must hold. In using the creed as a framework for teaching, post-Tridentine catechesis, while ostensibly following early Church tradition, was actually doing violence to it; for, as a matter of fact, it was not the creed but the creed-commandments-sacraments that formed the pattern of modern catechisms. This apparent addition was no improvement. Whatever the creed is, it certainly is not one-third of Christianity's teachings. The threefold division not only exhausts morality and liturgy of their doctrinal significance, inevitably reducing the former to ethics and the latter to ritual, but it utterly misconstrues the nature of the creed.

If creeds have any part to play in structuring religion teaching, they must become what they were for the early Church: the communal expression of the whole Christian faith, every line of which is morally and liturgically significant. For a time in the catechetical movement some people thought it important to rearrange the order of the catechism from creed-commandments-sacraments to creed-sacraments-commandments. It soon became evident, however, that although the latter is better than the former, both are so at variance with the nature of Christian revelation that the gain from such a change is trivial. Some recent catechisms and textbooks (for example, the German National Catechism) have attempted to reintegrate their whole presentation within a creedal framework. Whether they are wholly successful in this attempt is another matter. More important still, whether the significance of such a change will be seen by teachers depends upon their own orientation and their understanding of revelation. In the hands of poorly prepared teachers, the best catechisms in the world remain inadequate instruments.

The attitude of prayerful obedience within the totality of faith can and must be carried over to all of the authoritative teaching

111

of the Church's magisterium. This teaching comes from within the "mystery of faith" and represents a true but always partial penetration of the meaning of revelation. Rather than present official teachings of the Church as fetters upon the free inquiry of the Catholic, the catechist should strive to show how such teaching frees the individual from his own arbitrariness, thus setting him to deeper thinking within the community. Belief is always a communal act; a "private" Christian belief is almost a contradiction in terms. The individual receives his faith in bearing witness within a Church to which alone was promised the fullness of faith. "The great theologian is the entire Church, the Christian people. It is such in the measure in which it believes and thinks in union with Him who is the Truth, and not through some prodigious feat of universal suffrage."[13] Those who are entrusted with authoritative teaching in the Church do not derive their office and power from the consent of the faithful, nor is their teaching based upon the vote of the majority. There is an *ecclesia docens* and an *ecclesia discens,* but it would be inaccurate neatly to separate people into one of those two categories. All in the Church are listeners and learners, including the pope and college of bishops. All are teachers of the faith, though all do not do it in an official capacity.[14]

Doctrinal teaching in the Church is not a sign from above to stop thinking below. No question is simply ended by the fact that authority has spoken, though a definite direction to future thinking may have been given. Formulas expressive of the Church's faith, although they be valid and truthful, are always in principle replaceable by better formulations. Indolent teachers like to think that their job is finished once they have presented

[13] Mersch, *Theology of the Mystical Body,* p. 21.

[14] See *Constitution on Divine Revelation,* Chapter II, Article 10; see also Robert Murray, "Collegiality, Infallibility and Sobornost," in *One in Christ,* I (1965), 19–42; John L. McKenzie, *The Power and the Wisdom* (Milwaukee, Bruce, 1965), pp. 178–190.

the dogmatic definition and deduced some conclusions. Good teachers have always recognized that a "de-finition" does just that: sets out a framework for fruitful thinking. A teaching of the Church, even when infallible, is a fragmentary truth which should act as a prod to theologians and faithful alike to begin thinking more deeply on the subject in question.[15]

The catechist who engages the Church's teaching in the historical context of its development will neither belittle nor exaggerate the significance of these pronouncements. Formulas such as are used in catechisms cannot be eliminated, but they must be constantly reëxamined and always situated within their proper context. Doctrinal statements are as exposed as scriptural ones to being taken as truths handed down from the heavens without human reception and interpretation. They ought, instead, to be seen as means to prevent misunderstandings and as objectifications of what has been assimilated in the Church's experience. Given that context, their inherent limitations will also be apparent.[16]

The tendency to treat revelation as the collection of doctrinal truths taught in religion class will persist as long as little children are forced to learn formulas which are quite meaningless to them. A reduction of religion teaching to the inculcation of the catechism combined with a somewhat irrational desire to teach as many doctrines as possible to young children cannot end any other way than in a mutilation of true understanding, a boredom with religious ideas, and an emergence of verbalism and formalism. According to Catholic teaching, the child is already in grace and faith; teaching brings to reflexive consciousness and under-

[15] See Karl Rahner, "Current Problems in Christology," in *Theological Investigations,* I, pp. 149–153; Hans Küng, "Freedom and Theology," in *Social Digest,* VIII (January, 1965), pp. 10–11; Edward Schillebeeckx, "Exegesis, Dogmatics and the Development of Dogma," *loc. cit.,* pp. 124–125.
[16] See Barbotin, *loc. cit.,* p. 29; Van Caster, *op. cit.,* p. 102.

standing the revelation already given fundamentally. Since this is true, it is exceedingly difficult to understand why anyone should object to letting the child grow up into the understanding and vocabulary of doctrinal pronouncements in a way that is consonant with his nature and general growth pattern.

The whole structure of Catholic doctrine must eventually emerge in balanced perspective with each truth measured against the whole. The teacher must be especially careful in treating highly controversial matters lest some small truth appear to be of paramount importance. We are aware today that one can do a disservice to the truth while making true statements. The general catechetical attitude cannot be polemical or defensive. The orientation of the teaching must be reflective of the movement toward greater unity that characterizes revelation. If truth and knowledge are understood to surpass all human statements, there will be less temptation to create a system of truths that would in practice replace revelation. The teacher within the Church must be confident of the truth which he speaks and yet modest in his proposal of each individual statement of truth. Above all, the catechist must be a learner, one who is always seeking to further his own understanding, and who by contagion gives this attitude to his hearers. "Only that man is knowing who understands that he must keep learning over and over again and who above all, on the basis of this understanding, has attained to the point where he is always *able to learn*."[17]

The teaching of all doctrine must spring in some way from human life and be reflected in it at every moment. Nothing is more offensive to the present generation of students and nothing is more useless to Christian revelation than the maintenance of a system of abstractly defined truths which bears neither examination in nor relation to the real world. The proof is in the

[17] Martin Heidegger, *An Introduction to Metaphysics* (New York, Doubleday Anchor Book, 1961), p. 18.

114

living. "We do not merely toss out dogmas to men who are crying out in dire need. We begin to teach Christian truth successfully by ourselves beginning to live for our fellow men. Our life must itself be the incarnation of what we believe, for only when dogmas are lived do they have any attractive power."[18]

[18] Schillebeeckx, *Christ the Sacrament of the Encounter with God*, p. 209.

X.

Revelation and Individual Freedom

In the previous chapters we have situated God's revelation in the history of the Christian community and have shown that holy Scripture and the Church's teaching form the interpretive norm of self and community understanding. The gift which God makes of himself to the Church and to the individual Christian precedes all preaching and catechizing. The revelatory communion of God and man is established prior to all catechetical instruction, so that the catechist can never conceive of his task as that of molding or forming a neutral object. Among Catholics it is believed that the child is in the "state of grace" after having received baptism. This means that the Spirit of God has worked a transformation which though beyond conscious awareness in the infant is a reality that is to be freely accepted later in life.[1] The Spirit who is the realization of God's personal love gives testimony within that we are the sons of God (Rom. 8:16). God calls man to a supernatural life and gives him the ability to live it.

Two immediate consequences of this theological fact are pertinent here. First, the human teacher is always subordinate to the Holy Spirit in the catechizing of the child. "Catechesis is not an

[1] See Schillebeeckx, *Christ the Sacrament of the Encounter with God*, p. 111.

116

event between the catechist and the child, but between God and the child."[2] Neglecting this fact, the teacher will either be affected with undue optimism, believing he can form another person into being a Christian, or else he will be cast down with pessimism on finding that, in fact, much of his work is, humanly speaking, worthless. The catechist ought to think of himself as a voice through which Christ can speak to his members. A teacher has neither the right nor the power to determine the religious life of another. However, it is precisely through recognition of his limitations that the catechist can see the greatness of his mission. He will not try to achieve many tangible and visible results, but will trust that his words and his life's testimony do affect the student at a deeper level.[3]

The second consequence of the Spirit's indwelling is that the child is capable of religious attitudes and actions beyond what adults may suspect. "Adults are inclined to regard the spiritual life and the desire for perfection as something beyond the child. This is due to lack of appreciation of the sacrament of Baptism. God moves freely in the world of childhood. Children thirst to know Him and to draw close to Him."[4] This does not mean that adults should set about to teach all kinds of doctrines and devotional practices to little children. On the contrary, it means that adults ought to be very wary of imposing external formalisms which do nothing but inhibit the work of nature and the Holy Spirit. The task of the adult is to listen to the Spirit and to guide the child by awakening his consciousness in the Spirit.[5]

[2] Franz Arnold, as quoted in Georg Hansemann, "Das Stundenbild der kerygmatischen Katechese," in *Christusverkündigung in der Schule,* p. 99.
[3] See Fargues, *op. cit.,* p. 16: "The educator often has a too conceited idea of his role. He is not the Holy Spirit: not much, nor even a little, he is not the supernatural agent of education, it is not up to him to give faith."
[4] Sofia Cavalletti and Gianna Gobbi, *Teaching Doctrine and Liturgy* (New York, Alba House, 1964), p. 56.
[5] See Oraison, *Love or Constraint,* p. 120; Mouroux, *From Baptism to the Act of Faith,* p. 46.

Everything in the child's early experience that contributes to his development as a human being is also a foundation for his adult Christian life. There can no longer be any doubt about the importance of the "education of the unconscious" and of creating the milieu in which the emotional responsiveness of the child can flower. This should always have been demanded by the nature of Christian revelation, but when revelation tended to be identified with concepts, propositions, and doctrines, it was supposed that early religious education was not very important. Our study of the theology of revelation joins forces with the findings of modern psychology in emphasizing the crucial significance of the budding religious life of the small child. The child absorbs his parents' attitudes toward specific things such as prayer. Even more broadly, the child's whole psychic orientation and his balance for living a mature religious. life depend quite largely upon the parents' exercise of authority, their kindness and patience, their thoughtfulness and understanding. One need not load down children with religious concepts that are likely to be misunderstood by them. It is enough to establish small children in a universe of Christian charity.[6]

The development of the child's religious life and the emergence of the presence of the Spirit into reflexive consciousness is mediated by all of the child's relationships with the world. It is primarily through contact with other people that he can discover the attributes of God and the characteristics of Christian revelation. There is no way to explain to a small child what it means

---

[6] See Oraison, *Love or Constraint,* p. 97: " 'If you are not good you will hurt Baby Jesus . . .' A monstrous lie: this will hurt Daddy or Mama, perhaps, but 'Baby Jesus' has nothing at all to do with the question. Surely it can already be of enough importance without directly implicating the suffering Christ for the child to learn to make an effort not to hurt a human being; quite simply, in other words, to exercise a still embryonic charity that is generously and duly considerate of the existence of 'another.' "

to be a Christian; it can only be demonstrated. Through contact with parents, teachers, and other Christians, the child should come to see that becoming a Christian means finding oneself in one's own ultimate truth. Especially with the young, but also with people of every age, there must be a communication of Christianity through the testimony of adult human lives. What is indispensable to religious education, therefore, is *witness*.

The Christian witness is one who allows "another to discover in the warmth of a sympathy full of respect and veneration something of God's love which will be a seed of the greater revelation of God's goodness and kindness."[7] This notion of the teacher as a Christian witness is a common one in catechetical writing today. I would agree that the role of the catechist is to be a witness. I would also point out two considerations which may seem too obvious for saying, but which I think need saying. First, the teacher is a witness by teaching. He is a witness in other ways, no doubt, but insofar as he is a teacher it is precisely by good teaching that he witnesses. The catechist who is serious about his Christian faith will prepare well his teaching and teach with skill, enthusiasm, and understanding. Any witnessing on the part of teachers that is offered as a substitute for competent teaching would have to be judged illusory. To imply that catechists can manage with little scriptural and theological preparation as long as they are good witnesses would be to travesty both teaching and witnessing. Teaching is not the whole of Christian witness nor the highest form of witness. It is a small but significant part of the total Christian witness. Let those who can take it, take it for what it is worth.

Second, the catechist in recognizing that he is nothing less than a witness must also recognize that he is nothing more. A

[7] Alfonso Nebreda, "Role of Witness in Transmitting the Message," in *Pastoral Catechetics,* p. 85.

witness is one who is severely limited in his means for moving others precisely because he recognizes the other as being other. The witness is one who recognizes and accepts the values of freedom and personal autonomy. His only means for transforming another person is an appeal to the freedom of the other. If this appeal does not seem to work, it cannot be put aside in favor of some other instrument. The catechist, like every other Christian, succeeds by being a witness to freedom or else he does not succeed at all.

We may take note here of the common division of catechetical "approaches" into four: Scripture, liturgy, doctrine, and Christian witness.[8] That these are avenues of communication for the teaching of religion is quite obvious. But this fourfold division used as the outline of *the* ways to teach religion or as the organizing principle of curriculums leaves much to be desired. In the first place, this division tends to cause a narrowing of outlook in the approach of the teacher. There are not four ways or four approaches to the teaching of Christianity; there are innumerable ways, many of them loosely structured ways. The approaches will multiply in the proportion that teachers are given adequate theological preparation. If teachers at present cannot be given such preparation, there is still no point in narrowing their minds into four categories. Second, the division is poor insofar as the categories are not all of the same kind. They overlap one another and provide no intelligible pattern for curriculum construction. Lumping together such diverse things under one heading tends to destroy the proper reality of each. In particular, I strongly doubt that the meaning of Christian witness comes through in this division. Witness is being trivialized into illustrative examples that are tacked on to Scripture, liturgy, and doctrine; or

---

[8] These four are formulated in the tenth of the basic principles stated at the Eichstätt Catechetical Congress of 1960; see *Teaching All Nations*, p. 399.

witness refers to the "social problems" one looks to after he has learned his revelation. But the witness of Christian life, far from being one of the four ways to teach about Christianity, is the continuing locus of all religion teaching.

The teacher's whole life and his contacts with the student ought to be a witnessing to the reality of God's revelation. He is a Christian teacher insofar as he achieves personal contact with the freedom of the individual where the decisive battle of Christianity is waged. Teaching excessively large classes or teaching in impersonal surroundings makes this kind of contact difficult, though not impossible, to attain. The teacher in all his attitudes and in every action affects the other in ways usually not apparent. A gesture, a smile, or a suggestion may have the most profound effect. The catechist testifies to the presence of the Spirit by showing that his whole life has been grasped by the Spirit of God. Without desiring to minimize the importance of educational apparatus and organization, we may still assert that the focal point of catechetical improvements ought to be the teacher and the apostolate of the witness.

The teacher need not worry nor should he feel slighted if all of his formal religion teaching and all his personal concern for the student seem to be fruitless while some other person's brief contact seems to awaken a Christian sense. In the last analysis, it is the Church of believers who witness and teach. Each person who is striving to be faithful to his Christian vocation exercises an influence beyond himself, often in ways that he never suspects. One of the specific characteristics of Christian witness, but one not always recognized, is that it must be a communal witness. In other religions and in other spheres of human existence, the individual's life can be a testimony to some value. Christianity, as the religion whose aim is to unite all men in charity, demands that the witnessing be at least implicitly a communal act. The individual must be as attentive to the Christian community in which he lives as to those he is trying to attract to it. The cate-chist in a school cannot rely solely on his own individual influ-ence with students, but must be mindful of the total impression that the school and the faculty of the school convey.

The relationship between persons that we call revelation is not an act of the intellect or of the will or a combination of the two, but an act of man at that level at which truth is not separ-able from freedom.[9] Every offer of love by a person is revelatory of himself and at the same time an invitation to the other to achieve his autonomy. Unless there is such an invitation and communication in men's lives they will never be freed from their fears and unconscious desires. To take a step beyond themselves, people need a faith by which they can affirm themselves. This is especially true of young people and adolescents, who have no fund of self-appreciation on which to rely. "They look for some-one who will believe in them. And for many of them the cate-chist's belief in them will be the only road to the realization that God 'believes' in them—believes in them infinitely more than even the best and most trustworthy teachers."[10]

The young person must be given the confidence to trust the human nature God has given him and to distrust any other in-dividual structure imposed upon his unique existence. When there is a readiness to receive what God gives him and to use it as best he can, a person's small failings are not serious and can be easily corrected. The teacher can be of help only if he is will-ing to accept the student as he is and help him to accomplish what is in fact possible for him at a particular moment. It is in the individual concrete existence that God's revelation happens. No catechist can ever claim to have spoken the revelatory word

[9] See Cirne-Lima, *op. cit.*, pp. 129–145.
[10] Eva Fleischner, "The Mystery of Christ and the Formation of the Catechist," in *Twenty-Fourth North American Liturgical Week. The Renewal of Christian Education*, XXVI (1963), p. 79.

because the conditions of a revelatory situation are beyond his control. What he can do is prepare the ground for allowing the student to hear God in the events of his life. The process may be a long and difficult one; some people may require specialized help. A person should not be abandoned because he cannot immediately fulfill all the demands of Catholicism.[11]

With everything that is said these days about personal influence in conveying God's revelation, it is perhaps necessary to voice one warning. It is possible to abuse personal influence just as it is possible to abuse authority and power. If the teacher is truly witnessing to God and at the same time revealing the student to himself, then there is no problem here. The stronger the personal influence and the deeper the personal relationship, the more luminous will be the revelation of God. But those who through their own persons try to reveal God to others are always in danger of standing in the way and of drawing men to themselves rather than pointing beyond themselves to the source of all attractiveness, power, and love. Even Paul and Apollo seem to have had some difficulty on this score.

If a child is too dependent upon the personal influence of parent or teacher for his religious beliefs and practices, this could have unfortunate results. When he is removed from them or when he outgrows a certain stage of hero worship, his religious life may crumble away. It may be a painful fact for some parents and teachers to accept, but education must mean growth in independence and freedom. The test for determining whether God's revelation is being mediated through the catechist is whether the student is growing toward an autonomy where he will no longer stand in need of the catechist.[12]

[11] See Rahner, "Men in the Church," in *Theology for Renewal,* pp. 68–78.

[12] See Vincent Ayel, "Professeur ou témoin?" in *Catéchistes,* XXIII (1955), p. 218; Andrew Greeley, "Authority and Freedom," in *Homiletic and Pastoral Review,* LXV (September, 1965), p. 1003: "It is so very easy

As I have previously pointed out, one can reach the freedom of another only indirectly. Every impatient attempt to mold the freedom of another is bound to fail. Recent catechetical literature claims that the teacher should not merely teach about God but should convey a direct knowledge of God, that the catechist should not just instruct but "enable the child to encounter God." Although there is a good intention behind such statements, there is also an utter failure to face the mystery of human freedom and the true significance of the catechist's work. Teachers are still being encouraged to say too many things with too many words and to make everything clear for the students that they may encounter God. This fails to grasp the fact that effective religious instruction works indirectly, and that it therefore "should be more reserved in sharing the mystery. . . . Much should be taught only in parable, that they 'will hear and not hear.' "[13]

Many words will not make up for past words which have not been spoken. Many words will not provide them with what they should receive in the future but might not receive. God reveals himself not in the unending flow of words from the lips of the catechist, but in the calm and gentle exchange between persons. "It is silence that makes speech personal. Without it, dialogue is impossible. But in a revealed religion, silence with God has a value in itself and for its own sake, just because God is God. Failure to recognize the value of mere being with God, as the

---

for a priest or religious who is dealing with young people to exploit the young person's inclination to hero worship some of the adult figures in his life. They are so pathetically eager to please us while we are their heroes that we can have great influence on them and persuade ourselves that we're doing much good work with them. The influence does not last and the good work comes to an end but it is quite simple to tell ourselves that they did not have the gift of persevering in following our good advice. The fault, then, is theirs, not ours."

[13] Goldbrunner, "Catechesis and Encounter," *loc. cit.*, pp. 34–35.

Beloved, without doing anything, is to gouge the heart out of Christianity."[14]

I would call into question the frequently repeated principle that the teacher must always be seeking a response and that nothing should be taught which does not elicit a response. This could be a correct principle based upon a theological understanding of revelation that demands a participating subject. But if insufficiently understood or badly applied, this could be a most harmful principle. Certainly, it should not be interpreted simplistically to mean that everything that is taught to young people will have or should have some immediate and direct reaction in their lives. Worst of all would be the supposition that the teacher can intend and plan to have the student respond to and encounter God as if there were some way that a human being could directly cause this in another. The reserve needed here is well stated by Goldbrunner: "That the student follow the educator and teacher, falling freely into the guiding movement, that is, showing forth discipleship, allowing himself to be led—to cross over—all this can only be longed for, hoped for, prayed for. If at the end 'theocentric crossing' (conviction, transference) has been effected, it is a gift, grace, meeting of providence and freedom. It happens suddenly and unsystematically but may never be pitted against intentionally organized education and instruction."[15]

It is highly dubious advice to suggest to religion teachers that they have present to their minds a knowledge aim and a conduct aim for each lesson. The really deep values of Christian revelation are those that emerge organically over a long period of time. The attempt to make it a conscious and deliberate response too

[14] Schillebeeckx, "The Church and Mankind," loc. cit., p. 99; see also Joachim Jeremias, The Central Message of the New Testament (New York, Scribner's, 1965), pp. 88–90.
[15] See "Catechesis and Encounter," loc. cit., p. 33.

quickly destroys the possibility of its ultimate development. To introduce "moral applications" into every lesson and every discussion is certain to be artificial and to create a deadening effect. Few things are more repulsive to the present generation than constant exhortations to practice virtue, to give good example, and to use our fellow men as targets for virtuous acting. There is a sense in which the catechist must not care what his results are, must not look for nor desire an easy acceptance of what he is teaching. Immediate and visible success is not the sign of authenticity in catechetical work. The true test of catechizing is whether the work endures in time and is ultimately creative of freedom.

In this way the catechist is saved from propagandizing or trying to persuade people by mass suggestion and trick advertising. The very thing that Christianity can never admit, namely, that the individual is but an object to be handled and controlled by another, is not always avoided in the work of preaching and catechizing. This is due in part to the failure to recognize that there are in the contemporary world many ways besides physical coercion to violate personal freedom. It is also due to the fact that pre-personal techniques may appear to achieve a desired good end in a short time. Admittedly, there is much both within and without a classroom that necessarily occurs on a pre-personal level. For example, there are some rules of order that must be maintained even if not every individual freely consents to them. But ultimately pastoral and catechetical work must be concerned with the free, personal center of man which can only be appealed to but never forced or tampered with. Any playing upon the sensibilities of children is a form of manipulation unworthy of human beings. Sentimentalism is an affront to the revelation of God which is considered insufficiently attractive and powerful to create a religious life for students. What is needed in opposition to this is not a barren rationalism which tries to live on

ideas alone, but free and creative personalities who have inte-
grated emotional response and intellectual understanding into
human and religious activity.[16]

Christianity, if ever there was one, is the religion for adults.
When lived by children it must be lived as "on the way." Their
religion can only be lived according to the limited possibilities
available at each stage of their development. They should not be
subtly encouraged, let alone pressured, to take up practices which
are not authentic expressions of their own religious lives. It is to
be feared that much of what is supposedly religious practice on
the part of children is nothing more than a façade which will create difficulties in years to come. They should be allowed to grow
up and to discover their freedom through a process involving repeated effort, occasional fall, and renewed attempt. The acceptance of the divinely established principle of freedom means that
there is a risk inherent to the process. To give people the capacity
to say yes entails the possibility that they may say no. The catechist must face this fact squarely lest he panic at the first misuse
of freedom.[17]

Christianity is the religion that demands an absolute commitment of human freedom. Only he who is ready to give up his
life for Christ can find his life in Christ. Freedom and salvation
come with the recognition and acceptance of an absolute who
stands in no need of us though we stand in desperate need of
him. Because of the nature of man as historical being, and in
addition because of the sinfulness of the human world, a decision

[16] See Jacques Audinet, "La démarche de l'appel des valeurs," in *Catéchistes,* LIV (April, 1963), p. 150.
[17] See Brother Philippe André, *loc. cit.,* p. 337: "Christ's is a catechesis
sensitive to human liberty, but it is also a pressing appeal to this liberty
to commit itself. The divine principle remains unchanged. Christ proposes,
He does not impose, Himself. He plays the great game of freedom to the
hilt. He accepts all its risks and knows that it can result in the apparent
failure of His action."

127

of complete acceptance of the Christian life is impossible before there is a certain maturity of age and experience. No *a priori* rule can be stated for determining when an individual reaches such a point. Generally speaking, it is probably later in life than has usually been assumed.[18]

The forcing of a supposed commitment upon the child or adolescent when he is not yet capable of sustaining it is one of the most disastrous procedures in religious education. Not only may the catechist be deceived into thinking that he has formed a Christian, but what is worse, the young person himself may think that he has finally discovered Christianity when in fact he is mixed up in romanticism and hero worship. Of such commitments, Lee correctly notes, "the emotional immaturity and instability that makes it possible to achieve it fairly easily is the very reason why it is premature."[19] Life must be kept multi-dimensional and polyphonous. Adolescents must learn to think from various perspectives and to choose beyond the worlds of illusion that their intense private feelings construct. Into this turbulent eruption of flesh and psyche Christian revelation cannot be inserted as the answer to their problems nor as the primary motivation for their actions. Christianity can only be the ultimate option that lies beyond the immediate physical and psychological struggles, not the answer to their problems nor an escape from their problems, but the ever calm invitation to find themselves and the real world of God and people by trust and by a love that overcomes fear.

A total commitment for a youth yet incapable of it is both illusory and dangerous. By forcing such a commitment, parents, preachers, and catechists only succeed in creating new problems

[18] See Babin, *Crisis of Faith,* pp. 100–121; and his "The Faith of Adolescents toward the End of School," in *Religious Education,* LVII (March, 1962), pp. 128–131.

[19] See *Your Growing Child and Religion* (New York, Macmillan Paperback, 1963), p. 215.

which the young person must face when his idealistic outlook no longer sustains the self-committal. At that point he may struggle through the challenge which would have been better faced earlier, or he may reject his religion as something suitable for children and idealistic adolescents. The one other alternative is that he will settle into a comfortable "realism" in which he carefully preserves "revealed doctrines" and pious practices for one compartment of life while he seeks to enjoy the rest of life in morally neutral fashion. This last position is perhaps the worst one for it is an inhuman condition in which the gift of freedom is not faced. The situation of such a man is worse than that of someone who consciously believes that he can no longer remain within the Church, but who with his whole life is still seeking the God of Christian faith.

What is at stake, therefore, at every moment of human life is *freedom,* the ultimate mystery of the creature who can either give himself to or refuse himself from the one who is the presupposition and end of his existence. Man is free in the act of and to the extent of accepting God. For revelation to become the full divine-human meeting it is meant to be, there must be a freedom presupposed which becomes more fully itself as it exercises its power to discover the living God. There could hardly be a worse miscalculation than to think that a student can be taught God's revelation before any respect is shown for his own freedom.

Catholic religious education, therefore, is not the formation of one person by another along precise and rigid lines of what constitutes the ideal life. It is rather the guiding of a partner in conversation to discover what he alone can discover and what he alone can put into operation. God reveals himself in the bodily, personal, social existence of men. Though the Church is divinely guided to provide the framework within which the search takes place, God means something different for every man. God's love is directed not toward universal natures but to concrete existents.

Catechists should hardly be surprised if the Catholicism which emerges in the life of the student is not at all points identical with the ideal image in the head of the catechist. The catechist must recognize the importance of his work in the total revelatory process while realizing that he has not the capacity to produce a life of Christian freedom from the outside. "All one can do to teach this liberated freedom of the individual is to exemplify it, in a way which awakens in other people, by a mysterious sympathy, the courage to take hold on their own uniqueness."[20]

[20] Karl Rahner, "The Christian Teacher," in *Theology for Renewal*, p. 117.

XI.

Revelation and Man's World

THE Christian student, as other men, can find God through a so-called general or natural revelation. The whole created universe has always revealed something of God to man. Although modern technology has tended to make man feel less responsive to God in nature, those who are ready to listen can still hear God speak to them through creation. Christian faith retains its natural foundation which prevents its degenerating into an irrational leap that would be destructive of reason. A study of the natural foundations of faith remains a valid undertaking; but apologetic presentations of an earlier age, formulated almost exclusively in static and impersonal modes of thought, prove quite inadequate today. Furthermore, it is doubtful whether the proper catechetical approach was ever to try to separate the student's faith from his reason and to appeal to the latter alone. It must be remembered that the student is not a neutral observer of the universe and of religious faith. The believer cannot pretend that he is not a believer so as to argue himself back into belief.

The dissatisfaction of students with the typical proofs of apologetics books does not so much imply the need for better formulated and more up-to-date proofs as a reorientation of thinking on faith, personal decision, and Christian revelation. It is a fact that Catholic theology legitimately distinguishes between natural and supernatural revelation. This distinction does not solve their relationship, however, it only poses the problem. Even on the theoretical level there is not the neat division which most text-books have implied. In the personal existence of the individual the interrelationship is incomparably more complex. It is of some note that the *Constitution on Divine Revelation* takes in the whole sweep of revelation without a prior distinction of natural and supernatural revelation.[1] The catechist in presenting revelation to the young should follow this lead, neither denying the difference between natural and supernatural nor beginning with their distinction. When a sharp dichotomy of the two orders is made at the start, the result is a superficial extrinsicism that simply juxtaposes the two without understanding the question of their relationship. Thus we get a theory of grace as a "second storey on nature."

The scriptural presentation of creation as an inner element in the total revelation is not a naïve conception to be explained away by theologians and catechists. The creation of the world is not simply a past "natural" fact preceding supernatural revelation, but a present happening in the concrete historical structure of personal existence. As I have maintained, the only place at which one can begin catechizing is the real student who lives in relationship to a present community and to God. Too early a distinction between natural and supernatural revelation, something that is not at all evident in the student's experience, unnecessarily confuses matters.[2]

The personal relationships that actually structure the individual's life ought never to be disregarded. The appeal to a field

[1] See *Constitution on Divine Revelation,* Chapter I.

[2] For the question of the relationship between natural and supernatural in Catholic theology today, see Karl Rahner, *Nature and Grace* (New York, Sheed and Ward, 1964), pp. 114–143; and the same author's "Concerning the Relationship between Nature and Grace," in *Theological Investigations,* I, pp. 297–318.

132

of pure nature (where theoretically all men would agree) as either the original basis of faith or a buttress to faith in crises has little to recommend it. It is far better to start with the admitted position and the actual experience of the student working within faith to examine the rational basis of faith. To give students the impression that they cannot be sincere believers unless they accept certain rational proofs which prescind from their actual Christian lives is dangerous business. It could do untold harm by putting them into an intolerable position. On the one hand, they may see that the discovery of many of these proofs has followed, not preceded, the acceptance of Christian revelation. On the other hand, they may find the proofs compelling for a while and then be badly confused when they later find that the proofs are unconvincing apart from Christian revelation.

What must be made clear at all times is that it is the fullness of human life and not just man's syllogisms that open out to faith and revelation. Reason must not be forced to accept something above itself, nor is reason to be overwhelmed by some proof or fact that sacrifices intellect to a realm other than itself. Human reason and experience must grow and expand to the point of seeing that the acceptance of reason demands an opening of reason beyond itself. In the midst of individual crises of faith, especially during adolescence, the only direction to go is forward toward the further enriching of human experience. God cannot be brought in as a concept which completes an argument. He is not a piece of this world but its presupposition. He must emerge at the center of human life. God will be God for adult Christians only in their accepting and living to the full their present experience of a world which cannot be written off and a humanity which cannot be short-circuited.

The end which God has determined for man affects him in the actual, concrete structure of his personal existence. The fullness of revelation-redemption in Christ implies that all mankind has a

133

relationship to the Son through the action of the Spirit. This transforming work of the Spirit affects man's world and social organizations, a fact which becomes continually more important. "In Christ and through him, human existence has become the objective expression of God's absolute communication of himself to man and, by the same token, the objective expression of the human response to that total divine gift."[3] Embedded in the social milieu, the expression of this divine communication has become the mental horizon in which every individual exists. It is not only the baptized Christian to whom God speaks from within life, but every man who lives in this "christic" world. Every religious approach to man, every deliverance of a personal message, every act of fidelity, love or courage, is a movement toward bringing to awareness one's own "salvation history."[4]

The whole of man's world is expressive of God's revelation in Christ. Nothing of itself is guaranteed to be a revelatory instrument, but everything by the grace of God has become capable of being revelatory of the Christian God. This fact opens unlimited possibilities for the teaching of Christian revelation. When it is proposed that the grace of Christ is awakened by the catechist's words, this does not mean that it is only "religious" concepts and words which are in question. Any words, ideas, pictures, or experiences which create the possibility of deep personal reflection can have a place in catechetical instruction. Words and activities with no apparent religious orientation may be all the more powerful by reason of the indirectness of the appeal. The catechetical movement has not even begun to come to grips with this most fundamental issue. With few exceptions, catechetical literature and religion textbooks with the "new approach" are blunted in their effectiveness by their unending flow of religious ideas and words.

[3] Schillebeeckx, "The Church and Mankind," *loc. cit.*, p. 81.
[4] Rahner, *Nature and Grace*, p. 100.

My perspective here as elsewhere in this work is not psychological but theological. It is precisely a theology of revelation that demands a broader human base from which catechetical work can proceed. Because God's revelation is to transform man and because God is speaking now to man, every activity that is truly humanizing has an inner relation to Christian revelation. It is unthinkable, for example, that the forms of contemporary art, the developments in scientific technology, and the productions of modern literature do not bear trace of God's revelatory activity. Movements to establish the human rights of every person—even if the movements have non-religious sources—cannot be considered extraneous to God's revelatory activity. Good teachers, of course, have always used the "secular instruments" of the day for teaching religion, but they have generally viewed this as a tactical necessity rather than as a demand of Christian revelation itself.

Students should come to see that the Church exists as in a diaspora. Whatever be the reason or the culpability for this situation, it is the given fact to be recognized and accepted today.[5] The Church of the diaspora is the vanguard of God's revelation of the ultimate unity and love of mankind. The Christian can neither retreat from his mission to the world nor can he simply identify himself with the world. He must seek to find God in the events of world history among men who do not even suspect God's presence. This implies for the Christian a life of tension, working for a reconciliation which cannot be achieved in his lifetime, but which is the common work of mankind. Christian revelation and the human sciences are not the same thing, but they do meet in man. A strong opposition between a scientific-cultural community centered upon man and a Christian com-

[5] See Karl Rahner, "The Present Situation of Christians: A Theological Interpretation of the Position of Christians in the Modern World," in *The Christian Commitment*, pp. 3–37.

munity centered upon God would not be acceptable to a Catholic understanding of revelation. In every age Christian revelation must be formulated anew not only on the basis of past documents, but in relation to the present cultural context. This cannot be accomplished without a knowledge of the sciences so influential in determining our present culture. There are no substitutes for the knowledge and techniques that are necessary to understand this world in which revelation happens. The Christian must reach out toward the whole of mankind and to the limits of the universe, for he knows that ultimately the whole of mankind is to be united in the charity of Christ.

The task for our students, then, is not to dominate or condemn the world, but to serve God through helping man and giving witness to the reality of Christ's love. If they understand what Christian love means and what it demands in their own lives, they will be ready to work in an ecumenical spirit with all men of good will. Because Catholicism rightly understood is broad enough and bold enough to assume into itself all that is truly human, the student's faith will not be threatened by indifferentism nor be defended by an artificially contrived apologetic. Both the individual and the Church are bound today to the mission of studying and interpreting, of speaking and listening to, of teaching and learning from, both Christian and non-Christian religions.

These considerations lead me to a word which has recently become popular in catechetical writing, that is, "pre-evangelization."[6] What has been described under this term by writers such as Liégé and Nebreda bears strong similarity to some of what I have advocated above. There are several points, however, that I

[6] For the meaning of pre-evangelization, see Nebreda, *Kerygma in Crisis,* and also the articles of Nebreda previously cited (consult Bibliography). My criticism which follows is not meant as an attack upon Nebreda; I would hope that Nebreda would agree with the general line of this criticism.

136

would like to make with reference to this recent development.

The need for a stage called "pre-evangelization" was first real-ized in missionary countries, particularly in the Far East, where the culture of the countries differed radically from the "Christian West." Speaking from the background of his experience in Japan, Nebreda writes: "If you start by presenting the Christian fact, you sense somehow that the audience feels as if you were talking to somebody else. They remain untouched. The words they hear mean little or nothing to them. They do not feel themselves challenged."[7] Nebreda thus urges that before the gospel preach-ing there be a new kind of apologetics for "the creation of a vital and personal contact, an atmosphere in which a truly human dialogue can take place."[8]

It is now being said in many quarters that the students we have in our schools are in a state similar to pagan lands, that they too cannot understand the message and must be put through a stage of pre-evangelization or pre-catechesis. This is only partly true. There are vast differences between the problems of the missionary apostolate and the problems of catechizing in coun-tries long affected by Christianity. It is hardly to the point to gloss over all the differences with statements such as "every country is mission land today." In many respects the problems are exactly opposite, that is, we suffer not from a lack of acquaintance with and a scarcity of relationships to Christianity, but from an oversaturation (without accompanying assimilation) of Chris-tian ideas and words. It is not that our students have never heard about Christian revelation; many are sick to death of hearing about it. The introduction of a new artificial stage in which one pretends that none of this has happened or that one can start all over is not likely to help.

The most serious danger here is that, because of a misunder-

[7] See *Kerygma in Crisis,* p. 46.
[8] *Ibid.,* p. 106.

standing of Scripture which springs from a naïve conception of revelation, what is called pre-evangelization will be equated with pre-Christianity. I do not think that the work of the catechist, therefore, is being clarified. He is simply being encouraged to use some psychological tools to get his hearers ready. When they are prepared for it, he gives them the real Christian message, that is, the truths of Scripture and Christian doctrine. This is the same narrow approach to conveying "Christian truths," only now prepared for by psychological spadework. All that this will mean to many people is that the famed "kerygmatic approach" has not worked and that we are thus returning to apologetics at a slightly more sophisticated level. So long as theorists spend most of their time discussing how many stages there are and what to name them, such reactions are inevitable.

I do not deny that the missionary apostolate has much to offer to our understanding of the catechetical task, but the connection between these two lies not in the idea of stages or in the new words, but in the theology which underlies them. This is the real significance of the missionary experience, that is, in freeing us from a verbalized and propositional revelation and in making us come to grapple with a present, personal, and social revelation. Unfortunately, however, it is this very theology which is not fully developed. I would therefore agree with Nebreda that "one of the most urgent needs of the Church today is to elaborate, on sound theological grounds, the meaning and role of pre-evangelization in transmitting the message."[9] Without such theological development the newest literature on "pre-evangelization" is already threatened with a degeneration into jargon, gimmicks, and new rigidity of approach. More articles on the meaning of pre-evangelization will avail little. What is desperately needed is good Catholic theology which will give support to both missionary and catechetical work without getting entangled in these categories.

[9] *Ibid.*, p. 66.

What ought to have become clear through the missionary experience and in the catechetical movement is that God reveals himself in the real existence of present communities. Christianity claims that the fullness and perfection of that revealing take place in the humanity of the risen Christ. Holy Scripture as the privileged testimony to that revelation in Christ has a unique role to play in the interpretation of the revelation that happens in every human life. God's revelation, however, is not the same as holy Scripture, and the fact that Scripture has not been introduced does not mean that revelation is absent. Every inquiry based on Christian love is a searching into revelation; every genuine exchange between men that works toward the perfection of the human community already involves Christian revelation. Men do discover and assent to God's revelation without the Scriptures being proclaimed; or else we would have to assume that the vast majority of men have no way to make an act of saving faith.

I would therefore challenge such statements as "Man cannot discover the message of salvation, which is a divine revelation, on his own. It must be announced, proclaimed, transmitted as Word of God, under his mandate."[10] Man, of course, does not discover God's revelation on his own. He discovers God because God has first discovered him, and he finds God's revelation not privately but through the human community. But that he cannot find God's revelation until it is announced and proclaimed to him is a different question. Some people may find the revelation of God coincidental with its announcement and proclamation. For most people, however, it would seem that they have begun to discover the God of Jesus Christ in the love of a human being, in the joyful face of a believer, or in the secret longings of their own hearts. The verbal deliverance of the message will help to clarify these experiences and bring into explicit and reflexive

[10] Josef Goldbrunner, "Catechetical Method as the Handmaid of Kerygma," in *Teaching All Nations*, p. 112.

139

consciousness their knowledge of the Christian God. This thesis is not meant to deëmphasize the role of holy Scripture. On the contrary, it is meant to underline the fact that Scripture can enter the process at any point and is not to be given some one spot in a new but still rigidly conceived pattern. A great concern with the stages and divisions in contemporary catechetical work is distractive and irrelevant. If one likes, he can rightly call a certain element in the teaching process "pre-evangelization," but what is far more important is to find some teachers who have an understanding of Christian revelation and its place in our world.[11]

A better understanding of the theology involved here would also make clear why dialogue and discussion in religion class not only are not excluded but are the heart of the process. It has frequently been said that "discussions are necessarily limited because the content of Revelation cannot be won through conversation, discussion, co-operation; it must be heard and accepted by a believing heart."[12] With the first half of this statement I flatly disagree. Revelation must be heard and accepted by a believing heart, but it is given to man in personal existence by the Spirit of God and not by any human teacher. Why do catechetical writers

[11] A good theological perspective is provided by Joseph Bournique, "Note on Pre-Evangelization," in *Teaching All Nations,* II (January, 1965), pp. 96–97: He points out that (1) the world in which we live is not pure nature, man is always more than man; (2) there are traces of likeness to God that are not erased by sin; (3) "Every man is given over to his incompleteness and his intrinsic contradictions so long as he has not reached the level of Jesus Christ. On the other hand every effort to bring human life into line with true nature brings man closer to Christ, for nature is called to higher things." Pre-evangelization in this context is (1) a necessary dimension of all evangelization; (2) not necessarily first chronologically although there may be a long preliminary stage; (3) a form of evangelization which is (a) *implicit* though directed to the proclamation of salvation in Jesus Christ, (b) *partial* but conducive to global adherence to the fullness of mystery, (c) *attentive* to signs that are human realities and which lead to discovery of the plan of God.

[12] Ferdinand Kopp, "Discussion Techniques," in *New Catechetical Methods,* p. 97.

140

not take seriously their own profession that the content of revelation is Jesus Christ instead of immediately reverting to the implicit identification of revelation and Church doctrines? I have affirmed at length the role of authoritative teaching in the Church, but this authority is exercised from within the dialogue of God and the community. Such authority not only allows but demands conversation, discussion, and cooperation.

I would claim, therefore, that there is *no other way* to revelation than to discover it as a "given" in one's own life. The best way in which the meaning of this revelation will be clarified is through a teaching that always includes a dialogic element. Every effective teacher takes his hearers into at least an implicit dialogue with himself even when he lectures. Jesus did not exempt himself from this style of teaching even though he surpassed all other teachers in the authority of his teaching.[13] He knew, just as every competent religion teacher knows, that the student must discover revelation in dialogue with others if it is to be truly his own. There is nothing arbitrary or haphazard in this conception of revelation. This would be so only if one were to confuse intelligent discussion and dialogue with a group of people giving forth ungrounded opinions. A competent teacher brings to the discussion his own understanding and a preparation of the students so that the result is not whimsical. The teacher and the students are engaged in a serious intellectual inquiry searching for the meaning of God's revelation in their lives. They are part of the whole Church which is always searching for what God is now offering, now asking. And while it would be senseless to neglect the authoritative witness of Scripture and Church teaching, it remains true that no statement of Scripture or Church can give them the answer which would end the need for discussion.

[13] See Alonso Schökel, *op. cit.*, pp. 321–322; Congar, *Jesus Christ*, p. 59; Reuel Howe, *The Miracle of Dialogue* (Greenwich, Seabury Press, 1963), p. 41.

I have said that revelation is an intersubjective communion and that there is no revelation unless God is revealing and man is believing. This is to be distinguished from the supposition that revelation consists of external events juxtaposed with an inner light. This common presentation of revelation does not overcome the subject-object dichotomy.[14] The failure to face this issue usually results in revelation becoming identified with the "outer object." Even at present there is an unceasing tendency in Catholic theology toward a radically objectivist notion of revelation.

In no place was this objectivist bias clearer than in the traditional catechism. Here the revelation of God comes to be equated with precisely worded statements. The "revealed truths" are inculcated as early as possible to offset dangerous and erroneous thinking. The catechism, writes Marie Fargues,[15] is based upon the supposition and the fear that the child is naturally subjectivist, radically critical of all evidence. This, she goes on to point out, is a groundless fear because the normal attitude of the child is to trust the word of the educator.

During adolescence, it is true, there is a movement toward a subjectivism in piety.[16] This may be dangerously egocentric and quite at odds with the objective structure of the Church. But to meet this problem with a highly objectified picture of God's revelation is hardly a solution. The bare demand that adolescents accept a vast collection of doctrines and practices may make them feel they can no longer live in the Church. Christianity must rather be understood as concerned primarily with people rather than things, and not isolated individuals but the community of persons sharing in God's life. The adolescent crisis of faith would not thereby be resolved, but at least it would be

14 See Moran, *Theology of Revelation*, pp. 171–178.
15 *Op. cit.*, pp. 32–33.
16 See Pierre Babin, *Faith and the Adolescent* (New York, Herder and Herder, 1965), pp. 41–55.

correctly situated. Within the revelational process there are objective elements that the adolescent must grow to accept, but it should at least be made clear to him that Christianity is capable of bearing within itself ideals of moral perfection and subjective experience of religion.

In the overcoming of the split between subject and object, catechists are often more aware of the problem than theologians. Some catechetical writers have recognized that a deeper synthesis is needed within which subjective and objective elements are partial aspects. Marcel van Caster, in particular, has seen that there can be no question of juxtaposing the cognitive and volitional, the intellectual and sensible, the subjective and objective.[17] He proposes a synthesis of these elements in what he calls "initiation," a word which in English leaves much to be desired. At any rate, he does place at the center the interpersonal union of God and man upon which we have based our theology and catechesis of revelation. Van Caster conceives of catechetical procedure in steps which form a cyclical rhythm: a global phase, an analytical phase, and a new synthesis. This, it seems to me, is basic to setting up curriculums for religion teaching. If there must be a general pattern or plan, then the teaching ought to begin with the concrete experience of the student, proceed to some analysis and clarification, and return to the total personal level again. I would add that the initial step could include almost anything in the Christian life and that the clarification of experience, while utilizing the interpretive norms of Christian revelation, could be variously structured and sometimes almost completely lacking in logical pattern.

Discussions on setting up a religion curriculum usually presume that there is a "content" on one side and children on the other, and the problem is to match one with the other. It is then assumed that one must choose to construct the curriculum theo-

[17] See *op. cit.*, pp. 12–21.

logically according to the content or psychologically according to the children. This conception is not entirely accurate. We are not forced to make such a choice, a fact that renders the problem simpler but incomparably more difficult to handle. It is true that there is a distinction between the people who are the Church and the objective elements which are inherent to the Church. But the distinction is one between poles in a single revelatory process and not between people and revelation. There is no revelation except in God revealing himself in personal experience. In deciding upon the basis of a religion curriculum it simply is not true that one should choose (or could choose) either the child or the revelation. One must choose to structure it according to the people precisely because that is where revelation is. The whole content, I repeat, is found in Jesus Christ and Christians.

The above is not to be misrepresented to mean that the objective elements of Christian revelation are to be disregarded. They are to function in teaching as they function in revelation, that is, they are the means to understand God's revelation as it happens in human life. But it is life and revelation that are to be understood. Neither should the above be understood as an advocacy of "problem-centered" teaching constructed around the "needs" which the students claim to have.[18] An aimless and endless discussion of the students' "problems" (sex, drinking, parental authority, etc.) does not meet their real need. To give the formation of the curriculum over to the students is an abdication of adult authority and responsibility. The basis of the curriculum is the students precisely insofar as they are confronted with God's revealing of himself in the human community of past and present.

[18] See Sherrill, *op. cit.,* p. 181: "This does not mean that we must always have a specific 'problem' in view whenever a portion of Biblical material is selected. When man is confronted by the living God something will be said to *him,* and often enough it will have nothing to do with the question which he brought with him into the encounter. It may be a wholly new question which he for his part must now answer."

Genuine dialogue has nothing to do with pandering to every adolescent fancy. It means confronting the adolescents with the real world against which they can cut their teeth. The purpose of a religion curriculum is simply to set the learners in relation to that world through the use of human intelligence and genuine adult authority.

This principle does not solve the problems of setting up programs of religious instruction, but it casts doubt on many proposed schemes. Curriculum designers, even when enthusiastic over Scripture and liturgy, are still conceiving of a body of things somewhere outside people which must all be gotten inside. The great inrush of Scripture and liturgy has not changed at all the underlying notion of Christian revelation: still things, not people.

The best that can be done for the present, it would seem, is to suggest some general categories in a curriculum within which teachers could work to create understanding of some aspects of Christian revelation. The fact that some parts of Christianity would be left out and some overlapping would occur is not the crucial point. What is important is to start looking to where revelation happens—in the student's experience of the present community—and to start trying to give him some help in making some sense out of his life by using his Christian understanding. For this, one needs teachers who have studied and lived Christianity on an adult level and are willing to take up the search anew with students.

XII.

Revelation to the End

THE final aspect of our study which throws light upon catechetical work is found in the ending of revelation on earth.
Studies of the past century have demonstrated that the future,
final revelation is not a mere appendage. Rather it is of the
essence of the Church to be looking forward to the final coming.[1]
Revelation as a human reality depends upon past and future for
its present meaning. Even beyond other realities in man's existence, the significance of revelation issues from man's intention
for the future and, more important still, God's intention. What
God's intention for the future is becomes clear only through
revelation in the risen Lord, but even then the detailed working
out of the future remains veiled to us.

Christian revelation does indicate to us that history is moving
toward a definitive point of presence, union, and charity. How
cataclysmic this parousial revelation will be cannot be clearly
determined by a study of revelation. There are trends today
toward the uniting of mankind in bonds of relationship that some
people hope are prefigurements of the completed Body of Christ.

[1] See Georg Moser, "The Gospel of Fulfillment," in *Teaching All Nations,* II (January, 1965), pp. 83–84; see also Durrwell, *The Resurrection,*
pp. 250–300; Hans Urs von Balthasar, "Some Points of Eschatology," in
Word and Redemption (New York, Herder and Herder, 1965), pp. 153–
157.

On the other hand, there are undeniably other forces which seem to be moving the human race toward a devastating calamity of self-destruction. The Christian has no facile answers to the outcome of these ambivalent developments in modern times. He recognizes only that the "final act" is always at hand, that there are no further stages of revelation to be reached, that in some way it is given to man to determine his destiny.[2] God has taken man into a definitive relationship whereby man's responses to God's acts of love help to create the future.

These considerations ought to be of some catechetical significance today. A concern with "last ends" only for the purpose of moralizing in catechetics badly misses the mark. Too much concern with the "physics" of the last things is likewise not to the point.[3] What should emerge from a presentation of revelation that points to final fulfillment is a sense of historical evolution together with an appreciation of man's vocation. What Christianity had always implied has now come to the forefront of human consciousness, namely, that the future is not a repetition of the past nor a plan mechanically applied by God. The future is the genuinely novel emergence of reality yet to be born through man's free responses to God. This implies that the Christian goes forth to the world not with a bag of answers from the past, but with a deep sense of responsibility for making present and future decisions in the light of the great monuments of human history and Christian tradition. Even the very young have some awareness today of man's responsibility for the future. Such an awareness should not be disregarded but heightened. The existence of the means by which man can quickly annihilate mankind gives

[2] See Jean Daniélou, *Christ and Us* (New York, Sheed and Ward, 1961), p. 175; Karl Rahner, "The Resurrection of the Body," in *Theological Investigations*, II, p. 213; Franz Mussner, *Christ and the End of the World* (Notre Dame, University of Notre Dame Press, 1965), pp. 9–11.

[3] See Moser, *loc. cit.*, pp. 87–89; Ladislaus Boros, *The Mystery of Death* (New York, Herder and Herder, 1965), pp. 134–135.

147

to this awareness of responsibility for the future a new meaning and seriousness.

While remaining in the dark as to what the immediate future will bring, the Christian works with the assurance of a final victory. He believes that we are already a saved people. "In its present stage, revelation is in fact authentic but still incomplete. It will only be at the parousia, i.e., at the moment of final intervention of Christ, that it will be absolutely clear in which way God will communicate Himself to us and what our quality of Christian means."[4] There is always the looking forward in catechetical work, the attempt to speak what is now meaningful while opening the door to wider and deeper meanings. The catechist, even as he tries to teach about God, must also make clear that he does not claim to possess God. The catechist, too, waits for God and is one with the student in historical progress toward God.

Christian revelation seen from the perspective of its conclusion shows that man is moving toward a transformation which will be the emptying out of his egocentricity. He is to be emptied of his own self-centeredness, for he is nothing of himself but receives everything from God. The perfection of his freedom lies in that mysterious fusion of action and passivity, wherein man ceases to struggle and simply accepts. The key word in overcoming the paradox of freedom is "responsibility." All trust in self-activity is illusory; it is to live "in the flesh." Man must first relax, let go, and accept all God's gifts in the Spirit. In this receptive attitude before God, man's life becomes one of active response. Our students should come to see that "our task is always the humble and courageous one of listening obediently and acting boldly."[5]

[4] Marcel van Caster "Man in the Presence of the Word of God," in *Faith and Commitment,* p. 241.

[5] Romano Guardini, *The Life of Faith* (Westminster, Newman, 1961), p. 106.

148

The supreme example of the human paradox is Jesus Christ, who is the revelation both of God's self-bestowing love and of man's readiness to be acted upon and led by the Spirit. It is by partaking in fellowship with this person that human reality finds its fulfillment of acceptance and response. The final truth of this complete acceptance is that life can be attained only at the price of the willingness to die. Every revelatory relationship is sustained only by the death to selfishness and egotism. When one of the revelatory partners is the absolute and holy God, man's decision of acceptance entails a purification which destroys his root selfishness. The pledge of man's love is the beginning of man's death. "Love is, of course, and remains the triumph over death, but that is not because it abolishes death, but because it is itself death. Only in death is the total surrender that is love's possible, for only in death can we be exposed completely and without reserve."[6]

Central to the final perfection of God's revelation is the personal character of the entire process. There is clearly a connection between the loss of the personal nature of Christian revelation and the reification of "last things." A revelation of objects on earth naturally issues in a reward of things in a place called heaven. There must be a rehabilitation of the personal character on both ends of the process. Man can no longer believe in anything else, nor should he be asked to. The Christian view of life is not a final possessing or looking at things, but an intersubjective communion that leads to personal and communal completion. Hans Urs von Balthasar has beautifully summarized this: "God is the 'last thing' of the creature. Gained, he is heaven; lost, he is hell; examining, he is judgment; purifying, he is purgatory. He it is to whom finite being dies, and through whom it rises to him, in him. This he is, however, as he presents himself to the

6 Boros, *op. cit.*, p. 47.

world, that is, in his Son, *Jesus Christ,* who is the revelation of God and, therefore, the whole essence of the last things."[7]

A personal and historical revelation unto the end is necessarily a social revelation, an aspect that must be central to catechizing today. Man's destiny has always been tied to the whole of mankind; Christian revelation could never have implied anything else. It has only been in our generation, however, that this fact has become inescapably clear. No Christian can strive for his own salvation while disregarding that of his brothers. This implies, on the one hand, the complete acceptance of the historical, social process as the locus of God's activity, a devotion without limits to the humanization of the world. But it also means—by that very fact—a refusal to identify any particular world picture or social structure with the kingdom of God. We work neither for the preservation of the remnants of an ideal society from the past nor for the establishment of the perfect society of the future. Instead we recognize that there is no Christian society here on earth that would be finished and perfect; but it is precisely because we have no blueprints for the perfect society that we can be fully committed to the human. We believe in man not because of what we hope man will accomplish; we believe in man because God believes in him.

All of these aspects of revelation are brought together in Jesus Christ. It is in him and through him that men are to be delivered from hatred and fear and are to live in personal and social communion. He is the "gathering of his brethren," the source of the true human community. Only through fellowship with Christ does man find revelation and salvation.[8] Man is called to grow rich in the humanity revealed by the God-man and to grasp that he is inwardly linked with every other consciousness. The union is of bodily resurrection into the Body of

---

[7] See "Some Points of Eschatology," *loc. cit.,* p. 154.
[8] See Boros, *op. cit.,* pp. 99–105.

Christ. It is man who dies and man who rises and man who is to be transformed and be available to others. Nothing human, nothing of man's bodily life in the universe, is foreign to the work of catechizing. All that removes the duplicity of word and action, all that integrates bodily experience into love for others, is preparation for the kingdom of God.

The molds into which catechetical material is carefully being poured are shattered by the fact that the Body of Christ is now being formed out of the stuff of man's world. In the next few years the catechetical movement must make a basic decision: whether to turn in on itself and its formulas in narrowly conceived catechetical journals, or to expand its vision by opening out to the whole of man's personal life. Catechetics is on the verge of its greatest breakthrough; it must not be frustrated by rigid new schema, categories, and approaches. The only thing which can save the catechetical movement from self-strangulation is to prepare teachers who have a theological understanding of Christian revelation.

151

Bibliography

BOOKS

AHERN, BARNABAS. *New Horizons. Studies in Biblical Theology.* Notre Dame, Fides Dome Book, 1965.

ALONSO SCHÖKEL, LUIS. *The Inspired Word.* Translated by Francis Martin. New York, Herder and Herder, 1965.

ATHILL, MOTHER EMMANUEL. *Teaching Liturgy in Schools.* Chicago, Fides, 1958.

AUBERT, ROGER. *Le problème de l'acte de foi.* 3rd edition. Louvain, E. Waring, 1958.

BABIN, PIERRE. *Crisis of Faith.* Translated by Eva Fleischner. New York, Herder and Herder, 1963.

———. *Faith and the Adolescent.* Translated by David Gibson. New York, Herder and Herder, 1965.

BARTH, KARL. *The Humanity of God.* Translated by John Newton Thomas and Thomas Wieser. London, Collins, 1961.

BOROS, LADISLAUS. *The Mystery of Death.* Translated by Gregory Bainbridge. New York, Herder and Herder, 1965.

BUBER, MARTIN. *I and Thou.* Translated by Ronald Smith. New York, Scribner, 1958.

BULST, WERNER. *Revelation.* Translated by Bruce Vawter. New York, Sheed and Ward, 1965.

CARTER, GERALD EMMET. *Modern Challenge to Religious Education.* New York, Sadlier, 1961.

CATHOLIC CATECHISM. Books I and II. Teacher's Book. Issued by Australian Bishops' Committee for Education. Sydney, E. J. Dwyer, 1962–63.

CAVALLETTI, SOFIA and GOBBI, GIANNA. *Teaching Doctrine and Liturgy.* Translated by Sister M. Juliana. New York, Alba House, 1964.

152

CERFAUX, LUCIEN. *Christ in the Theology of St. Paul.* Translated by Geoffrey Webb and Adrian Walker. New York, Herder and Herder, 1959.

CHENU, M. D. *Is Theology a Science?* Translated by A. H. N. Green-Armytage. New York, Hawthorn Books, 1959.

CIRNE-LIMA, CARLOS. *Personal Faith.* Translated by G. Richard Dimler. New York, Herder and Herder, 1965.

COLLINGWOOD, R. G. *The Idea of History.* Oxford, Clarendon Press, 1946.

CONGAR, YVES. *The Meaning of Tradition.* Translated by A. N. Woodrow. New York, Hawthorn Books, 1964.

———. *Jesus Christ.* Translated by Luke O'Neil. New York, Herder and Herder, 1966.

CULLY, IRIS. *The Dynamics of Christian Education.* Philadelphia, Westminster, 1958.

DANIÉLOU, JEAN. *Christ and Us.* Translated by Walter Roberts. New York, Sheed and Ward, 1961.

———. *The Salvation of the Nations.* Translated by Angeline Bouchard. Notre Dame, University of Notre Dame Press, 1962.

DAVIS, CHARLES. *Theology for Today.* New York, Sheed and Ward, 1962.

DIRECTOIRE *de pastorale catéchetique à l'usage des diocèses de France.* Paris, Editions Fleurus, 1964.

DODD, C. H. *The Apostolic Preaching and its Developments.* 3rd edition. London, Hodder and Stoughton, 1963.

DONDEYNE, ALBERT. *Contemporary European Thought and Christian Faith.* Translated by E. McMullen and J. Burnheim. Pittsburgh, Duquesne University Press, 1958.

———. *Faith and the World.* Translated by Walter van de Putte. Pittsburgh, Duquesne University Press, 1963.

DRINKWATER, F. H. *Telling the Good News.* London, Macmillan, 1960.

DULLES, AVERY. *Apologetics and the Biblical Christ.* Westminster, Newman, 1963.

DURRWELL, F. X. *The Resurrection.* Translated by Rosemary Sheed. New York, Sheed and Ward, 1960.

———. *In the Redeeming Christ.* Translated by Rosemary Sheed. New York, Sheed and Ward, 1963.

153

ELIADE, MIRCEA. *Cosmos and History.* Translated by Willard Trask. New York, Harper Torchbook, 1959.

FARGUES, MARIE. *Catéchisme pour notre temps.* Paris, Editions Spes, 1951.

FRANK, ERICH. *Philosophical Understanding and Religious Truth.* New York, Oxford University Press, 1945.

GOLDBRUNNER, JOSEF. *Holiness is Wholeness.* Translated by Stanley Godman. New York, Pantheon Books, 1955.

———. *Individuation.* Translated by Stanley Godman. New York, Pantheon Books, 1956.

———. *Cure of Mind and Cure of Soul.* 2nd edition. New York, Pantheon Books, 1958.

GORDON, GLADYS. *Let's Be Catechists.* Paris, National Center of Religious Education, 1962.

GRASSO, DOMENICO. *Proclaiming God's Message.* Notre Dame, University of Notre Dame Press, 1965.

GROSSOUW, WILLIAM. *Revelation and Redemption.* Translated by Martin Schoenberg. Westminster, Newman, 1955.

GUARDINI, ROMANO. *Die Offenbarung.* Würzburg, Werkbund Verlag, 1940.

———. *The Lord.* Translated by Elinor Castendyk Briefs. Chicago, Henry Regnery Co., 1954.

———. *The Life of Faith.* Translated by John Chapin. Westminster, Newman, 1961.

———. *The Humanity of Christ.* Translated by Ronald Walls. New York, Pantheon Books, 1964.

HEIDEGGER, MARTIN. *An Introduction to Metaphysics.* Translated by Ralph Manheim. New York, Doubleday Anchor Book, 1961.

———. *Being and Time.* Translated by John Macquarrie and Edward Robinson. London, SCM Press, 1962.

HOFINGER, JOHANNES. *The ABC's of Modern Catechetics.* New York, Sadlier, 1962.

HOWE, REUEL. *The Miracle of Dialogue.* Greenwich, Seabury Press, 1963.

HUNTER, DAVID. *Christian Education as Engagement.* Greenwich, Seabury Press, 1963.

JACOB, EDMOND. *Theology of the Old Testament.* Translated by A. Heathcote and Philip Allcock. New York, Harper and Brothers, 1958.

JUNGMANN, JOSEF. *Handing on the Faith.* Translated by A. N. Fuerst. New York, Herder and Herder, 1959.

——. *The Good News Yesterday and Today.* Translated by William Huesman. New York, Sadlier, 1962.

——. *Pastoral Liturgy.* New York, Herder and Herder, 1962.

KAPPLER, EMIL. *Die Verkündigungstheologie.* Freiburg, Schweiz, Paulusverlag, 1949.

KIERKEGAARD, SØREN. *Concluding Unscientific Postscript.* Translated by David Swenson. Princeton, Princeton University Press, 1941.

——. *The Point of View for My Work as an Author.* New York, Harper and Row, 1962.

LA BONNARDIÈRE, XAVIER. *Devoir de croire et sincérité intellectuelle.* Paris, Aubier, 1949.

LANCE, DEREK. *Teaching the History of Salvation.* Glen Rock, Paulist Press, 1964.

LATOURELLE, RENÉ. *Théologie de la révélation.* Bruges, Desclée de Brouwer, 1963.

LEE, R. S. *Your Growing Child and Religion.* New York, Macmillan, 1963.

LEVIE, JEAN. *The Bible, Word of God in Words of Men.* Translated by S. H. Treman. New York, P. J. Kenedy and Sons, 1961.

LEWIS, EVE. *Children and their Religion.* New York, Sheed and Ward, 1962.

LIÉGÉ, PIERRE-ANDRÉ. *Consider Christian Maturity.* Translated by Thomas Donlan. Chicago, Priory Press, 1965.

LONERGAN, BERNARD. *Insight.* New York, Longmans, Green, 1957.

LUBIENSKA DE LENVAL, HÉLÈNE. *The Whole Man at Worship.* New York, Desclée, 1961.

MARCEL, GABRIEL. *The Philosophy of Existentialism.* Translated by Manya Harari. New York, Citadel Press, 1962.

——. *Homo Viator.* New York, Harper Torchbooks, 1962.

MARÉCHAL, JOSEPH. *Le point de départ de la métaphysique.* Cahier V. Paris, Desclée de Brouwer, 1949.

MCBRIDE, ALFRED. *Catechetics.* Milwaukee, Bruce, 1966.

MERSCH, EMILE. *Theology of the Mystical Body.* Translated by Cyril Vollert. St. Louis, B. Herder, 1951.

MONDEN, LOUIS. *Sin, Liberty and Law.* Translated by Joseph Donceel. New York, Sheed and Ward, 1965.

155

MORAN, GABRIEL. *Scripture and Tradition.* New York, Herder and Herder, 1963.

———. *Theology of Revelation.* New York, Herder and Herder, 1966.

MOUROUX, JEAN. *The Christian Experience.* Translated by George Lamb. New York, Sheed and Ward, 1954.

———. *I Believe.* Translated by Michael Turner. New York, Sheed and Ward, 1959.

———. *The Mystery of Time.* Translated by John Drury. New York, Desclée, 1964.

———. *From Baptism to the Act of Faith.* Translated by Sister M. Johnice and Sister M. Elizabeth. Boston, Allyn and Bacon, 1964.

MUSSNER, FRANZ. *Christ and the End of the World.* Translated by Maria von Eroes. Notre Dame, University of Notre Dame Press, 1965.

NEBREDA, ALFONSO. *Kerygma in Crisis.* Chicago, Loyola University Press, 1965.

NEWMAN, JOHN HENRY. *A Grammar of Assent.* Garden City, Doubleday Image Book, 1955.

NIEBUHR, H. RICHARD. *The Meaning of Revelation.* New York, Macmillan, 1962.

NOVAK, MICHAEL. *Belief and Unbelief.* New York, Macmillan, 1965.

ORAISON, MARC. *Love or Constraint.* Translated by Una Morrissey. Glen Rock, Paulist Press, 1961.

PIEPER, JOSEF. *Belief and Faith.* Translated by Richard and Clara Winston. New York, Pantheon Books, 1963.

RAHNER, KARL. *Theology of Death.* Translated by Charles Henkey. New York, Herder and Herder, 1961.

———. *Inspiration in the Bible.* Translated by Charles Henkey. New York, Herder and Herder, 1961.

———. *Theological Investigations.* Vol. I. Translated by Cornelius Ernst. Baltimore, Helicon, 1961.

———. *The Christian Commitment.* Translated by Cecily Hastings. New York, Sheed and Ward, 1963.

———. *On Heresy.* Translated by W. J. O'Hara. New York, Herder and Herder, 1964.

———. *Nature and Grace.* Translated by Dinah Wharton and G. Richard Dimler. New York, Sheed and Ward, 1964.

———. *The Dynamic Element in the Church.* Translated by W. J. O'Hara. New York, Herder and Herder, 1964.

————. *Theology for Renewal.* Translated by Cecily Hastings. New York, Sheed and Ward, 1965.

RAMSEY, IAN T. *Religious Language: An Empirical Placing of Theological Phrases.* London, SCM Press, 1957.

RÉTIF, ANDRÉ. *Foi au Christ et mission.* Paris, Les Editions du Cerf, 1953.

RICHARDSON, ALAN. *History Sacred and Profane.* Philadelphia, Westminster, 1964.

ROBINSON, JAMES M. *A New Quest of the Historical Jesus.* London, SCM Press, 1959.

ROUTLEY, ERIK. *The Man for Others.* New York, Oxford University Press, 1964.

RYAN, MARY PERKINS. *Are Parochial Schools the Answer?* New York, Holt, Rinehart and Winston, 1964.

SCHELKLE, KARL HERMANN. *Discipleship and Priesthood.* Translated by Joseph Disselhorst. New York, Herder and Herder, 1965.

SCHILLEBEECKX, EDWARD. *Christ, the Sacrament of the Encounter with God.* Translated by Paul Barrett. New York, Sheed and Ward, 1963.

————. *The Layman in the Church.* Translated by M. H. Gill and Son. New York, Alba House, 1963.

SCHMAUS, MICHAEL. *Katholische Dogmatik.* Band I. München, Hueber, 1960.

————. *The Essence of Christianity.* Translated by J. Holland-Smith. Chicago, Scepter, 1961.

SEMMELROTH, OTTO. *The Preaching Word.* Translated by John Jay Hughes. New York, Herder and Herder, 1965.

SHERRILL, LEWIS. *Gift of Power.* New York, Macmillan, 1955.

STRUNK, ORLO. *Religion: A Psychological Interpretation.* New York, Abingdon Press, 1962.

URS VON BALTHASAR, HANS. *Science, Religion and Christianity.* Translated by Hilda Graef. Westminster, Newman, 1958.

————. *A Theology of History.* New York, Sheed and Ward, 1963.

————. *Word and Revelation.* Translated by A. V. Littledale with Alexander Dru. New York, Herder and Herder, 1964.

————. *Word and Redemption.* Translated by A. V. Littledale with Alexander Dru. New York, Herder and Herder, 1965.

VAN CASTER, MARCEL. *Structure of Catechetics.* Translated by Edward

BIBLIOGRAPHY

Dirkswager, Olga Guedetarian and Mother Nicolas Smith. New York, Herder and Herder, 1965.

VRIEZEN, T. C. *An Outline of Old Testament Theology.* Oxford, Blackwell, 1960.

ARTICLES

ALFARO, JUAN. "Persona y gracia," in *Gregorianum,* XLI (January, 1960), pp. 5–29.

———. "Cristo glorioso, revelador del Padre," in *Christus Victor Mortis.* Rome, Gregoriana, 1958. Pp. 22–70.

———. "Une dogmatique de la révélation," in *Sciences Ecclésiastiques,* XVI (May, 1964), pp. 351–357.

ALLEMAND, L. EDWARD. "The Christ Encounter," in *Worship,* XXXVII (June, 1963), pp. 412–417.

———. "The Catholic School and Commitment," in *Living Light,* II (Spring, 1965), pp. 24–30.

ARNOLD, FRANZ. "Faith as Assent and Commitment," in *Lumen Vitae,* XI (September, 1956), pp. 571–582.

AUDINET, JACQUES. "La démarche de l'appel des valeurs," in *Catéchistes,* LIV (April, 1963), pp. 141–150.

———. "Perspectives pour une catéchèse de l'Eglise," in *Catéchèse,* V (April, 1965), pp. 173–194.

AYEL, VINCENT. "Faut-il aller du concret à l'abstrait?," in *Catéchistes,* XIII (January, 1953), pp. 13–24.

———. "Teaching the Church to Adolescents," in *Lumen Vitae,* VIII (July, 1953), pp. 417–447.

———. "Professeur ou témoin?," in *Catéchistes,* XXIII (1955), pp. 211–218.

———. "Progressive Nature of Catechesis," in *Lumen Vitae,* XII (January, 1957), pp. 71–88.

AYMES-COUCKE, SISTER MARIA DE LA CRUZ. "Teaching the Very Young in Spirit and in Truth: Kindergarten, First and Second Grade," in *Modern Catechetics,* edited by Gerard S. Sloyan. New York, Macmillan, 1963. Pp. 102–124.

BABIN, PIERRE. "Réflexions pour la catéchèse et l'éducation chrétienne des adolescents," in *Documentation Catéchestique,* XLV (1959), pp. 19–30.

158

————. "The Faith of Adolescents toward the End of School," in *Religious Education*, LVII (March, 1962), pp. 128–131.

BARBOTIN, EDMOND. "Connaissance rationelle et éducation de la foi," in *Documentation Catéchestique*, XLVI (1960), pp. 27–34.

BARR, JAMES. "Revelation through History in the Old Testament and in Modern Theology," in *New Theology No. 1*, edited by Martin E. Marty and Dean G. Peerman. New York, Macmillan, 1964. Pp. 60–74.

BESNARD, ALBERT-MARIE. "Is Our Technical Civilization Open to the Gospel?," in *Lumen Vitae*, XIII (1958), pp. 600–621.

BOSS, GERHARD. "Wort und Brot," in *Katechetische Blätter*, LXXXVIII (1963), pp. 30–34.

BOURKE, MYLES. "The Eucharist in the Church," in *Twenty-Fifth North American Liturgical Week. The Challenge of the Council: Person, Parish, World*, XXV (1964), pp. 31–39.

BOURNIQUE, JOSEPH. "Note on Pre-Evangelization," in *Teaching All Nations*, II (January, 1965), pp. 92–97.

BROWN, RAYMOND E. "Does the New Testament Call Jesus God?," in *Theological Studies*, XXVI (December, 1965), pp. 545–573.

BUBER, MARTIN. "The Education of Character," in *Between Man and Man*. Boston, Beacon Paperback, 1955. Pp. 104–117.

BURGHARDT, WALTER J. "History of Catechesis II: Catechetics in the Early Church: Program and Psychology," in *Living Light*, I (Autumn, 1964), pp. 100–118.

BUTLER, SISTER MARY PIERCE. "Must We Teach Morality according to the Decalogue?," in *Worship*, XXXVII (April, 1963), pp. 293–300.

COLOMB, JOSEPH. "The Use of the Bible in Teaching the Church's Faith," in *Modern Catechetics*, edited by Gerard S. Sloyan. New York, Macmillan, 1963. Pp. 1–22.

CONGAR, YVES. "Bulletin de théologie dogmatique," in *Revue des sciences philosophiques et théologiques*, XXXV (1951), pp. 591–603.

COOKE, BERNARD. "The Problem of Sacred Doctrine in the College," in *Modern Catechetics*, edited by Gerard S. Sloyan. New York, Macmillan, 1963. Pp. 267–290.

————. "Catechesis of the Church," in *Religious Education*, LIX (March, 1964), pp. 149–161.

159

————. "Theology and Catechetical Renewal," in *Pastoral Catechetics*, edited by Theodore Stone and Johannes Hofinger. New York, Herder and Herder, 1964. Pp. 88–104.

————. "Word of God: Scripture and Sacrament," in *Proceedings: Tenth Annual Convention of the Society of Catholic College Teachers of Sacred Doctrine*, X (1964), pp. 122–138.

————. "Relevance in Religious Education," in *Living Light*, II (Summer, 1965), pp. 80–93.

COUDREAU, FRANÇOIS. "Introduction to a Pedagogy of Faith," in *Shaping the Christian Message*, edited by Gerard S. Sloyan. New York, Macmillan, 1958. Pp. 131–149.

————. "Bible and Liturgy in Catechesis," in *Liturgy and the Word of God*. Collegeville, Liturgical Press, 1959. Pp. 99–118.

————. "Celebration of the Word in Pastoral Catechetics," in *Living Light*, I (Autumn, 1964), pp. 28–39.

————. "The Place of the Paschal Mystery in Teaching the Catholic Faith," in *Living Light*, I (Winter, 1965), pp. 72–81.

CROWE, FREDERICK. "Complacency and Concern in the Thought of St. Thomas," in *Theological Studies*, XIX (March, June, September, 1959), pp. 1–39, 198–230, 343–395.

DANIÉLOU, JEAN. "Parole de Dieu et mission de l' Eglise," in *Le prêtre ministre de la parole*. Paris, Union des Oeuvres Catholiques de France, 1954. Pp. 41–56.

DAVIS, CHARLES. "Theology and its Present Task," in *Theology and the University*, edited by John Coulson. Baltimore, Helicon, 1964. Pp. 107–132.

DE HAES, PAUL. "The Presence of the Lord Christ," in *Lumen Vitae*, XX (September, 1965), pp. 435–450.

DULLES, AVERY. "The Theology of Revelation," in *Theological Studies*, XXV (March, 1964), pp. 43–58.

————. "Revelation and the Apostolate," in *Apostolic Renewal in the Seminary*, edited by James Keller and Richard Armstrong. New York, Christopher Book, 1965. Pp. 111–122.

DUMONT, C. "Unité et diversité des signes de la révélation," in *Nouvelle revue théologique*, LXXX (February, 1958), pp. 133–158.

DURAND, A. "La science du Christ," in *Nouvelle revue théologique*, LXXI (May, 1949), pp. 497–503.

ELCHINGER, A. "The Bible and Catechesis," in *Teaching All Nations*, edited by Johannes Hofinger. New York, Herder and Herder, 1961. Pp. 137–152.

FARLEY, EDWARD. "Does Christian Education Need the Holy Spirit? 1. The Strange History of Christian *Paideia*," in *Religious Education*, LX (September, 1965), pp. 339–346.

———. "Does Christian Education Need the Holy Spirit? 2. The Work of the Spirit in Christian Education," in *Religious Education*, LX (November, 1965), pp. 427–436.

FLEISCHNER, EVA. "The Mystery of Christ and the Formation of the Catechist," in *Twenty-Fourth North American Liturgical Week: The Renewal of Christian Education*, XXIV (1963), pp. 72–83.

FORTMANN, H. M. M. "Toward a Development of Faith by Means of Liturgical Life," in *Faith and Commitment*, edited by Mark J. Link. Chicago, Loyola University Press, 1965. Pp. 51–63.

FOX, DOUGLAS. "Biblical Myth and Christian Education," in *Religious Education*, LX (March, 1965), pp. 117–120, 135.

FRANSEN, P. "Toward a Psychology of Divine Grace," in *Research in Religious Psychology*. Brussels, *Lumen Vitae*, 1957. Pp. 7–36.

———. "Sacraments, Signs of Faith," in *Worship*, XXXVII (December, 1962), pp. 31–49.

GALLEGO, SATURNINO. "La teología peculiar del catequista," in *Sinite*, II (1961), pp. 43–58.

GALOT, JEAN. "Science et conscience de Jésus," in *Nouvelle revue théologique*, LXXXII (February, 1960), pp. 113–131.

GELINEAU, JOSEPH. "The Nature and Role of Signs in the Economy of the Covenant," in *Worship*, XXXIX (November, 1965), pp. 530–550.

GODIN, ANDRÉ. "Faith and the Psychological Development of Children and Adults," in *Faith and Commitment*, edited by Mark J. Link. Chicago, Loyola University Press, 1965. Pp. 123–137.

GOLDBRUNNER, JOSEF. "Catechetical Method as the Handmaid of Kerygma," in *Teaching All Nations*, edited by Johannes Hofinger. New York, Herder and Herder, 1961. Pp. 108–121.

———. "Catechesis and Encounter," in *New Catechetical Methods*, edited by Josef Goldbrunner. Translated by Sister M. Veronica Riedl. Notre Dame, University of Notre Dame Press, 1965. Pp. 17–38.

GRASSO, DOMENICO. "The Good News and the Renewal of Theology," in Josef Jungmann, *The Good News Yesterday and Today*. Translated by William Huesman. New York, Sadlier, 1962. Pp. 201–211.

———. "The Catechist as Witness," in *Worship*, XXXVIII (February, 1964), pp. 157–164.

GRAY, DONALD P. "Liturgy and Morality," in *Worship*, XXXIX (January, 1965), pp. 28–35.

GREELEY, ANDREW. "Authority and Freedom," in *Homiletic and Pastoral Review*, LXV (September, 1965), pp. 999–1004.

GRILLMEIER, A. "The Figure of Christ in Catholic Theology Today," in *Theology Today:* Volume I: *Renewal in Dogma.* Translated by Peter White and Raymond Kelly. Milwaukee, Bruce, 1965. Pp. 66–108.

HANSEMANN, GEORG. "Zügange und Schwierigkeiten bezüglich der Christusverkündigung beim Schulkind der Gegenwart," in *Die Christusverkündigung in der Schule.* Köln, Verlag Styria, 1963. Pp. 43–62.

———. "Das Stundenbild der kerygmatischen Katechese," in *Die Christusverkündigung in der Schule.* Köln, Verlag Styria, 1963. Pp. 93–106.

HILSDALE, PAUL. "Superman versus Christ–God versus Demi-God," in *Living Light*, I (Winter, 1965), pp. 18–30.

HITZ, PAUL. "Théologie et catéchèse," in *Nouvelle revue théologique*, LXXVII (November, 1955), pp. 897–923.

HOLSTEIN, HENRI. "Faut-il un programme ou des centres d'intéret?," in *Catéchèse*, V (October, 1965), pp. 415–432.

HONORE, JEAN. "Les trois types de catéchèse christologique," in *Catéchèse*, II (October, 1962), pp. 425–440.

JUNGMANN, JOSEF. "Theology and Kerygmatic Teaching," in *Lumen Vitae*, V (April, 1950), pp. 258–263.

KIESLING, CHRISTOPHER. "The Liturgy in the Modern World," in *Chicago Studies*, IV (Spring, 1965), pp. 3–17.

KOPP, FERDINAND. "Discussion Techniques," in *New Catechetical Methods*, edited by Josef Goldbrunner. Translated by Sister M. Veronica Riedl. Notre Dame, University of Notre Dame Press, 1965. Pp. 82–97.

LABELLE, JEAN-PAUL. "The Use of the Bible during the Pre-Catechumenate," in *Teaching All Nations*, II (July, 1965), pp. 309–319.

LEVIE, JEAN. "Le message de Jésus dans la pensée des apôtres," in *Nouvelle revue théologique*, LXXXIII (January, 1961), pp. 25–49.

LIÉGÉ, PIERRE-ANDRÉ. "Contenu et pédagogie de la prédication chrétienne," in *La Maison Dieu*, 39 (1954), pp. 23–37.

LOHFINK, NORBERT. "The Inerrancy and the Unity of Scripture," in *Theology Digest*, XIII (Autumn, 1965), pp. 185–192.

LONERGAN, BERNARD. "Christ as Subject: A Reply," in *Gregorianum*, XL (1959), pp. 242–270.

———. "Cognitional Structure," in *Continuum*, II (Autumn, 1964), pp. 530–542.

MACE, ROGER. "Les miracles de l'Evangile dans l'enseignement religieux," in *Catéchistes*, LIII (January, 1963), pp. 63–74.

MARIE, FR. "El fin de la catequesis," in *Sinite*, II (1961), pp. 59–64.

MCCOOL, FRANCIS. "The Preacher and the Historical Witness of the Gospels," in *Theological Studies*, XXI (December, 1960), pp. 517–544.

MCNALLY, ROBERT. "Word of God and the Mystery of Christ," in *Worship*, XXVIII (June, 1964), pp. 392–402.

MENGS, IGNACIO. "Pastoral, predicación, catequesis," in *Sinite*, IV (1963), pp. 51–59.

MERSCH, EMILE. "The Teacher of Religion, His Interior Life and Teaching," in *Lumen Vitae*, XIII (January, 1958), pp. 19–32.

METZ, JOHANNES B. "Unbelief as a Theological Problem," in *Concilium*, Volume VI: *The Church and the World*. Glen Rock, Paulist Press, 1965. Pp. 59–78.

MOELLER, CHARLES. "Is It Possible, in the Twentieth Century, to be a Man of the Bible?," in *Liturgy and the Word of God*. Collegeville, Liturgical Press, 1959. Pp. 119–156.

MORAN, GABRIEL. "Faith as Aim in Religious Education," in *Catholic Educational Review*, LXI (February, 1963), pp. 113–121.

———. "Hope: Foundation of Religious Education," in *Catholic Educational Review*, LXI (May, 1963), pp. 302–312.

———. "Scripture-Tradition: Witness to Revelation," in *Continuum*, I (Autumn, 1963), pp. 343–354.

———. "Charity: Life of Religious Education," in *Catholic Educational Review*, LXII (March, 1964), pp. 158–168.

———. "The Freedom of the Sons of God," in *Twenty-Fifth North American Liturgical Week. The Challenge of the Council: Person, Parish, World*, XXV (1964), pp. 165–172.

———. "Freedom and Faith," in *Way*, XXI (June, 1965), pp. 36–41.

———. "Freedom in Christian Revelation," in *Proceedings: Eleventh Annual Convention of the Society of Catholic College Teachers of Sacred Doctrine*, XI (1965), pp. 59–79.

163

MOSER, GEORG. "The Gospel of Fulfillment," in *Teaching All Nations,* II (January, 1965), pp. 82–91.

MOUROUX, JEAN. "Connaître Jésus-Christ," in *Catéchèse,* II (January, 1962), pp. 409–424.

MURCHLAND, BERNARD. "An Awareness of Mystery," in *Apostolic Perspectives,* III (October/November, 1958), pp. 21–23.

MURRAY, ROBERT. "Collegiality, Infallibility and Sobornost," in *One in Christ,* I (1965), pp. 19–42.

NEBREDA, ALFONSO. "The Preparation of the Message," in *Faith and Commitment,* edited by Mark J. Link. Chicago, Loyola University Press, 1964. Pp. 186–203.

———. "Role of Witness in Transmitting the Message," in *Pastoral Catechetics,* edited by Johannes Hofinger and Theodore Stone. New York, Herder and Herder, 1964. Pp. 67–86.

———. "The Theological Problem of Transmission," in *Lumen Vitae,* XX (June, 1965), pp. 309–324.

NOVAK, VINCENT. "Teaching the Old Testament," in *The Bible Today,* I (April 1963), pp. 368–377.

O'NEIL, DAVID. "Catechism or Gospels?," in *Living Light,* I (Fall, 1964), pp. 88–98.

OSTER, HENRI. "God's Plan," *Readings in European Catechetics,* edited by George Delcuve and André Godin. Brussels, *Lumen Vitae,* 1962. Pp. 37–52.

PHILIPPE ANDRÉ, BROTHER. "Christ's Pedagogy in the Gospel," in *Modern Catechetics,* edited by Gerard S. Sloyan. New York, Macmillan, 1963. Pp. 323–345.

POTTEBAUM, GERARD. "Awakening the Young to God's Signs," in *Living Light,* II (Summer, 1965), pp. 36–43.

RAHNER, KARL. "Über die Wahrhaftigkeit," in *Katechetische Blätter,* (September, 1960), pp. 412–416.

———. "Christianity and Non-Christian Religions," in *The Church. Readings in Theology.* Compiled at the Canisianum. New York, P. J. Kenedy and Sons, 1963. Pp. 112–135.

———. "Priest and Poet," in *The Word. Readings in Theology.* Compiled at the Canisianum. New York, P. J. Kenedy and Sons, 1964. Pp. 3–26.

RICHARDSON, CYRIL. "Word and Sacrament in Protestant Worship," in *Ecumenical Dialogue at Harvard,* edited by Samuel Miller and G.

164

Ernest Wright. Cambridge, Harvard University Press, 1964. Pp. 152–171.

RIESENHUBER, KLAUS. "Rahner's 'Anonymous Christian,'" in *Theology Digest*, XIII (Autumn, 1965), pp. 163–171.

ROBINSON, JAMES M. "Scripture and Theological Method," in *Catholic Biblical Quarterly*, XXVII (January, 1965), pp. 6–27.

ROMERO, ANDRÉS A. ESTEBAN. "La controversia en torno a la teología kerigmática," in *XV Semana Española de Teología*. Madrid, 1956. Pp. 369–409.

RYAN, MARY PERKINS. "The Focus of Catechetics," in *Worship*, XXXVII (March, 1963), pp. 233–240.

———. "To My Critics," in *Ave Maria*, May 23, 1964, pp. 14–15, 25–26.

———. "The Christian and the Trinity," in *Twenty-Fifth North American Liturgical Week. The Challenge of the Council: Person, Parish, World*, XXV (1964), pp. 228–234.

SCHILLEBEECKX, EDWARD. "Revelation in Word and Deed," in *The Word. Readings in Theology*. Compiled at the Canisianum. New York, P. J. Kenedy and Sons, 1964. Pp. 255–272.

———. "Exegesis, Dogmatics and the Development of Dogma," in *Dogmatic vs. Biblical Theology*, edited by Herbert Vorgrimler. Baltimore, Helicon, 1964. Pp. 115–145.

———. "The Church and Mankind," in *The Church and Mankind*, edited by Edward Schillebeeckx. Glen Rock, Paulist Press, 1965. Pp. 69–102.

SCHREIBMAYR, FRANZ. "The Faith of the Church and Formal Doctrinal Instruction," in *Modern Catechetics*, edited by Gerard S. Sloyan. New York, Macmillan, 1963. Pp. 45–62.

SLOYAN, GERARD S. "The Relation of the Catechism to the Work of Religious Formation," in *Modern Catechetics*, edited by Gerard S. Sloyan. New York, Macmillan, 1963. Pp. 63–101.

———. "Catechetical Crossroads," in *Religious Education*, LIX (March, 1964), pp. 145–149.

———. "What Should Children's Catechisms Be Like?," in *Pastoral Catechetics*, edited by Johannes Hofinger and Theodore Stone. New York, Herder and Herder, 1964. Pp. 33–44.

———. "Teaching a Personal Relationship to the Father, the Son and the Spirit," in *Living Light*, II (Summer, 1965), pp. 22–34.

SOUFFRAY, JEAN-FRANCOIS. "Découverte de l'espérance chrétienne," in *Catéchistes*, XLVIII (October, 1961), pp. 331–338.

STANLEY, DAVID. "The Conception of Our Gospels as Salvation History," in *Theological Studies*, XX (December, 1959), pp. 561–589.

————. "The Concept of Salvation-History in the New Testament," in *The Bible Today*, II (March, 1964), pp. 686–693.

STUHLMUELLER, CARROLL. "The Prophet and the Word of God," in *Thomist*, XXVIII (April, 1964), pp. 133–173.

TAVARD, GEORGE H. "Scripture and Tradition: Source or Sources," in *Journal of Ecumenical Studies*, I (Autumn, 1964), pp. 445–459.

TILMANN, KLEMENS. "Bible, Source of Christian Doctrine," in *Lumen Vitae*, XII (September, 1956), pp. 605–616.

URS VON BALTHASAR, HANS. "The Freedom of the Subject," in *Cross Currents*, XII (Winter, 1962), pp. 13–30.

VAN BUREN, PAUL. "Christian Education Post Mortem Dei," in *Religious Education*, LX (January, 1965), pp. 4–10.

VAN CASTER, MARCEL. "Man in the Presence of the Word of God," in *Faith and Commitment*, edited by Mark J. Link. Chicago, Loyola University Press, 1964. Pp. 237–242.

WEIGEL, GUSTAVE. "The Meaning of Sacred Doctrine in the College," in *Shaping the Christian Message*, edited by Gerard S. Sloyan. New York, Macmillan, 1958. Pp. 170–182.

WOOD, GEOFFREY. "Man's Response to God's Word," in *The Bible Today*, II (December, 1963), pp. 573–579.

YEOMANS, WILLIAM. "You Shall be My Witnesses," in *The Way*, IV (January, 1964), pp. 24–32.

Index

169

Heresy, 24
Hilsdale, Paul, 59 n. 8, 162
History, 43–54; of the Church, 94, 116; of the Jews, 45, 50, 61, 85; of salvation, 22–24, 26, 43 f., 47, 53 f., 76 f., 90; of the student, 45 f., 48, 50 f., 52, 54 f., 80
Hitz, Paul, 28 n. 16, 162
Hofinger, Johannes, 154
Holstein, Henri, 162
Holy Scripture: see Bible
Holy Spirit, catechetics and, 40, 68, 73, 116 f., 118, 140 f.; indwelling of, 67, 116 f., 121, 149
Honore, Jean, 65 n. 19, 162
Hope, 52, 68
Hosea, 78
Howe, Reuel, 141 n. 13, 154
Humanism, 48, 53
Hunter, David, 18, 154

Indirect communication, 38 f., 124 f.
Indwelling: see Holy Spirit
Infallibility, 113
Initiation, 143
Inspiration, 78, 82
Intellectual understanding, 34–36, 69–73, 94, 96, 113, 119, 127, 141, 145
Interpersonal communion, revelation as, 13, 16, 27, 33, 50 f., 62 f., 68, 70, 79, 96, 142, 149
Isaiah, 47

Jacob, Edmond, 154
Jeremias, Joachim, 125 n. 14

Jesus Christ, 55–65; as center of catechesis, 26, 33, 55, 83 f., 86–88, 141, 144; as continuing mediator, 13, 54, 62, 65, 90, 92, 94, 101; as fullness of revelation, 16, 22, 24, 29, 55 f., 60, 66, 87 f., 149; as recipient of revelation, 13, 89; as Word of God, 60, 69, 77, 82; consciousness of, 60, 66; death of, 61, 63; divinity of, 56, 59; humanity of, 13, 16, 48, 59 f., 139; life of, 61, 88; resurrection of 13, 63, 92
Jews, and revelation, 16, 46, 48, 50, 55 f.
Job, 78
John, St., 15, 68
Joseph, St., 61
Judgment, 149
Jungmann, Josef, 20–27, 30 f., 93 n. 3, 95 n. 8, 155, 162

Kappler, Emil, 20 n. 2, 154
Kelly, J. N. D., 110 n. 12
Kerygma, 22, 30, 33, 37, 110 n. 12
Kerygmatic approach, 30, 138
Kerygmatic theology, 25–27, 30 n. 1
Kierkegaard, Søren, 38, 39 n. 9, 79 n. 4, 155
Kiesling, Christopher, 162
Knowledge, 23, 28 f., 72, 124, 136; in religion teaching, 35 f., 53 f., 57, 70–72, 103 f., 107–109, 113 f.; pre-reflexive, 69, 103, 116, 139
Kopp, Ferdinand, 140 n. 12, 162
Küng, Hans, 113 n. 15